Sir Isaiah Berlin OM was born in the Baltic city of Riga in 1909. In 1915 he moved with his family to Petrograd where, in 1917, he witnessed both Revolutions. In 1919 his family moved to England.

He was educated at St Paul's School and Corpus Christi College, Oxford. He was elected a Fellow of All Souls College (1932-38) where he is today, New College (1938-50), Chichele Professor of Social and Political Theory (1957-67) and first President of Wolfson College (1966-77). He was President of the British Academy from 1974 to 1978.

During the Second World War he was assigned to New York in 1941 by the Ministry of Information and in 1942 transferred to the Foreign Office where he served in the British Embassy in Washington until 1945 and then briefly in Moscow.

His intellectual achievements have earned him many honorary degrees as well as the Erasmus, Lippincott, Jerusalem and Agnelli Prizes.

Ramin Jahanbegloo is an Iranian philosopher who came to France in 1974. He is the author of *Hegel and the French Revolution* and is a frequent contributor to the French journals *Esprit, Croissance* and *Etudes*.

ALSO BY ISAIAH BERLIN

Karl Marx
The Age of Enlightenment
Four Essays on Liberty
Vico and Herder
The Hedgehog and the Fox

Selected Writings
Edited by Henry Hardy

Russian Thinkers
Concepts and Categories
Against the Current
Personal Impressions
The Crooked Timber of Humanity

Also by Ramin Jahanbegloo
Hegel and The French Revolution

Conversations with Isaiah Berlin

RAMIN JAHANBEGLOO

PHŒNIX

A PHOENIX PAPERBACK

First published in Great Britain in 1992
by Peter Halban Publishers Ltd

Copyright © Editions du Félin, Paris 1991

This paperback edition published in 1993 by
Orion Books Limited, Orion House,
5 Upper St Martin's Lane, London WC2H 9EA

The right of Ramin Jahanbegloo to be identified
as the author of this work has been asserted
by him in accordance with the Copyright, Designs
and Patents Act 1988

ISBN 1 85799 031 5

Printed and bound in Great Britain by
The Guernsey Press Co. Ltd, Guernsey, C.I.

British Library Cataloguing in
Publication Data available.

CONTENTS

❖

CONTENTS

SECOND CONVERSATION
The Birth of Modern Politics

THIRD CONVERSATION
Political Ideas: The Test of Time

CONTENTS

FOURTH CONVERSATION
A Philosophy of Freedom

FIFTH CONVERSATION
Personal Impressions

ACKNOWLEDGMENTS

❖

I would like to thank all those people who in various ways assisted me in my work on this book. In particular I would like to thank my friends Olivier Mongin, the Director of the journal *Esprit*, and Joël Roman, his Editor-in-Chief. The idea for such a book would never have taken shape without the friendly encouragement of Thierry Paquot and also the ideas and suggestions of my friend John Smyth. Similarly I am indebted to Mrs Pat Utechin, Isaiah Berlin's Secretary, for her invaluable assistance. I was supported and stimulated throughout the course of my work by my parents' encouragement and critical reading. I am greatly indebted to them for their example of strength and patience.

Lastly, I am grateful to John Murray Publishers, London, and to Alfred A. Knopf, Inc., New York, for permission to quote from *The Crooked Timber of Humanity* by Isaiah Berlin in my introduction.

R. J.

ACKNOWLEDGMENTS

I have enjoyed my talks with Mr Jahanbegloo, who has been a most courteous and patient interviewer. Mr Jahanbegloo has kindly allowed me to read his typescript before it went to press, and as is usual in such cases I wish to emphasize that responsibility for the precise form and cast of my words must lie with the author.

Isaiah Berlin
Oxford, November 1990

INTRODUCTION

❖

I first met Sir Isaiah Berlin on 6 June 1988, on his seventy-ninth birthday, in his apartment in the heart of London. The French translation of *Four Essays On Liberty*, one of the classic works of European political philosophy, had been well received by the French reading public. I had decided, therefore, to introduce Isaiah Berlin's thought to my colleagues at *Esprit* during a weekly literary seminar at the magazine's headquarters. The positive result of this meeting encouraged me to pursue my idea of presenting Isaiah Berlin's thought in more depth through an interview which *Esprit* agreed to publish. After a short telephone conversation with Isaiah Berlin and a rapid exchange of letters we decided to meet at his apartment. The idea of meeting a man whom I had admired for twelve years, ever since I discovered *Four Essays On Liberty* in Foyle's bookshop in London on a cold rainy day in January 1976, made me feel a little nervous. But when we first met he greeted me so warmly, with so friendly a smile, that my nervousness evaporated before I could even say a word.

As our talk began I tried to take in not only what Isaiah Berlin was saying but also how he looked. I had seen many photographs of him but nevertheless I was somewhat surprised by his actual appearance. His face at first glance did not suggest at all that of a man born in Riga. As he began to talk, his voice sounded precise and forceful, but his words were spoken slowly. His fully-accented Oxbridge English, which flowed rhythmically throughout our conversation, gave me the impression of having been admitted into the presence of a very distinguished British gentleman. But here was the most gentle and humble of men, speaking softly and in a kindly way, without the slightest pretence of trying to impress me. We talked together for over two hours. He gave me details of his childhood during the Russian Revolution and of his time at Oxford in the 1930s. I was also surprised by how close he felt towards Russian culture, having left Russia at the age of ten. When I left him that day I wanted to have another chance to see him again. But I had no idea that one day I would have the possibility of publishing these interviews in book form.

When I returned to Paris, I was contacted by an editor who asked me to continue with the interviews and to make a book out of them. I was happy to have another opportunity of meeting Isaiah Berlin. We met again in London in December 1988 and this time I had the honour of interviewing him on several different occasions. Each time the welcome was warm and friendly. I was able to ask him over 300 questions on his work in the field of the history of ideas, taking each subject and discussing it separately. He asked me to transcribe the interviews and I sent him the final manuscript. The book was published in France in January 1991.

Obviously, this book does not have the ambition of being the definitive biography of Isaiah Berlin. It could nevertheless stand as a major source for all that is yet to be written on him. There is sometimes a tendency to overestimate the importance of historians of ideas, but not with outstanding men such as Isaiah Berlin whose works have changed our sense of history and life; his impact on the intellectual and political views of the last fifty years in the English-speaking world alone makes it important to understand his works and analyse his thought. There are arguments and insights in his works that could help us to have a more critical view of concepts and events which have given shape to contemporary history. Therefore it seems undeniable that Isaiah Berlin's thoughts do present us with a challenge. Unquestionably at first glance he appears to be a typically distinguished Oxford philosopher of his generation. His Oxford philosophical background (making him a true admirer of Hume's philosophy), the great clarity of his thought and his extreme distaste for obscure terminology, make him a true representative of today's British philosophy. However, Isaiah Berlin is in some respects atypical of his intellectual generation. His entire philosophical experience could be examined as a theoretical battle against the belief that in principle there is a truth which is the one and only valid answer to the central problems of mankind throughout history. He rejects, therefore, the idea that a Utopia can be created on earth according to scientific, political or even aesthetic values. Given the fact that the history of mankind is the birthplace and the developing laboratory of values and ideals which always clash, Berlin traces the emergence of pluralism in the fields of ethics, politics and aesthetics. Knowing this, one can fully understand why, during the past fifty years, he has chosen the history of ideas as his centre of interest. For him this was undoubtedly the only way to throw light upon some of the crucial problems which have troubled him most deeply since his experience of the Russian Revolution as a child. The result of this approach has been a beautifully worded investigation of people's lives and thoughts that possesses all the literary qualities of a novel, while being at the same time a lucid and critical examination of historical ideas. What makes Berlin's essays so fascinating is that they are all written from an undogmatic point of view as they reveal to the reader certain of the author's preoccupations with perennial philosophical problems. Berlin is therefore not a Hegelian (or any other kind of) determinist, even if we can consider him a kind of phenomenologist of Western consciousness. Unlike the

Hegelian view of human history as a logical and ontological process of the development of Reason through pre-determined stages in history, ending in a conciliation between the real and the rational, Berlin's investigation pursues the various levels of the individual responsibility of philosophers, politicians and artists, which lead to the break-down of the metaphysical prison-house of historical inevit-ability. Hence, Isaiah Berlin is not interested in general attitudes and outlooks which end in a final solution. And as he argues in an essay published in his latest book, *The Crooked Timber of Humanity*:

... the very notion of a final solution is not only impracticable but, if I am right, and some values cannot but clash, incoherent also. The possibility of a final solution—even if we forget the terrible sense that these words acquired in Hitler's day—turns out to be an illusion; and a very dangerous one. For if one really believes that such a solution is possible, then surely no cost would be too high to obtain it: to make mankind just and happy and creative and harmonious forever— what could be too high a price to pay for that? To make such an omelette, there is surely no limit to the number of eggs that should be broken—that was the faith of Lenin, of Trotsky, of Mao, for all I know of Pol Pot. Since I know the only true path to the ultimate solution of the problems of society, I know which way to drive the human caravan; and since you are ignorant of what I know, you can not be allowed to have liberty of choice even within the narrowest limits, if the goal is to be reached. You declare that a given policy will make you happier, or freer, or give you room to breathe; but I know that you are mistaken. I know what you need, what all men need, and if there is resistance based on ignorance or malevolence, then it must be broken and hundreds of thousands may have to perish to make millions happy for all time. What choice have we, who have the knowledge, but to be willing to sacrifice them all?

When one gets closer to Isaiah Berlin's philosophical realm, one can understand much better why he invites us to read Herzen's *My Past and Thoughts*. The idea of "choice" is a key concept in both Herzen's and Berlin's intellectual outlook. When Berlin criticizes the Platonic ideal of the perfect life as the main texture of monism in Western thought, he is very close to Herzen who declares that "the ultimate goal of life is life itself" and "it is time to realize that nature and history are full of the accidental and senselessness, of muddle and bungling". In this sense, Berlin's heroes are people who refuse to see the world as a single, rational, harmonious, whole. This is the main reason why being close to the intellectual "currents" of eighteenth-century Europe —illustrated by the French *philosophes*—never hinders Berlin in bringing to light the life and thought of those thinkers who were against the "current". Once again Berlin's work in the history of ideas derives much of its force and value from its prevailing sense of freedom which is his main consideration when he approaches and praises the thought and general outlook of individuals who have boldly and openly fought against the dominant systems of rational thought. In doing this, Berlin shows us that there are no absolute values in history, and that history is all too full, with tragic consequences, of the agony of men who have tried to evade the tragic responsibility of choice by placing their faith in final and absolute truths.

Ramin Jahanbegloo
Paris, July 1991

FIRST CONVERSATION

❖

From the Baltic
to the Thames

THE TWO RUSSIAN REVOLUTIONS

RAMIN JAHANBEGLOO   First of all, I want to thank you for having accepted this interview. To start our discussion I would like, if I may, to ask you a few biographical questions about your past experiences and the influences that these might have had on your thought.

You were born on 6 June 1909, in Riga, and you left Russia with your parents at the age of ten. Do you still have memories of this period, in particular of the conditions of your immigration?

ISAIAH BERLIN   I left Riga with my parents for Petrograd[1] in 1915. We left Petrograd in 1919. In Petrograd I witnessed both the Russian Revolutions at the age of eight. I remember the First Revolution quite well. There were meetings, banners, crowds in the streets, enthusiasm, posters with the faces of the new Lvov[2] Ministry, propaganda by more than twenty parties for the Constituent Assembly. Not much talk about the war, at any rate in the circles in

---

1. St. Petersburg, founded in 1703 by Peter the Great, renamed Petrograd in 1914 before becoming Leningrad in 1924; renamed St. Petersburg in 1991.
2. The Provisional Government of Prince Lvov was shortlived (14 March to 25 July 1917). Kerensky, who succeeded him, had already assumed all power on 5 May.

which my family was living. The Liberal revolution was greatly welcomed by the Jews, and the liberal bourgeoisie. But this did not last long. The Bolshevik Revolution broke out in November. We—my family and its friends—hardly knew that it had happened. The first sign was a general strike against the Bolshevik seizure of power. Various newspapers disappeared. I remember there was a Liberal newspaper called *Day*—it reappeared as *Evening*, then as *Night*, then as *Midnight*, then as *Darkest Night*, and then, after four or five days or so, it was finally suppressed. There was distant shooting. People in our world thought that the *putsch* might last at most for two or three weeks. If you look at *The Times* of that date you will read reports from the Russian Ambassador in Paris: he predicted a quick end to the *putsch*. The Bolsheviks were called "Maximalists" in *The Times*, and not regarded as a major force. Gradually Lenin and Trotsky emerged as the two dominant figures of the Revolution. My parents, who were bourgeois liberals, thought that Lenin would create a society in which they would not be able to survive; they looked on Lenin as a dangerous fanatic but a true believer, honest and incorruptible, a kind of sea-green Robespierre. Trotsky, on the other hand, they regarded as a wicked opportunist. At the age of eight I had no idea why this difference between them was so strongly felt. They were never referred to apart—"Lenin and Trotsky" were spoken of in one breath like the name of a firm. The only people who remained loyal to the Tsarist government, I recollect, were the police. I do not think that there is much about this in the literature. The police in the streets were called Pharaohs—oppressors of the people. Some of them sniped at the revolutionaries from rooftops and attics. I remember seeing a policeman being dragged off, pale and struggling, by a mob, obviously to his death—that was a terrible sight that I have never forgotten; it gave me a lifelong horror of physical violence.

R. J.   Did you have problems leaving Russia after the Revolution?

I. B.   No. My family came from Riga, which became the capital of an independent state[3]. If you could prove that you were a native of Latvia, they let you go. We left Russia for Latvia. My father was a timber-merchant, who supplied sleepers for the Russian railways. For two years he continued to work for the new Soviet Russian Government, but in the end evidently could not bear it. We were never touched: neither my father nor any immediate member of my family was arrested or in any way molested. I remember people standing in queues for bread, or anything they could get: I was left standing to keep a place in such queues for four or five hours on end. A soup kitchen next door to our street provided some food, and there was a small cinema which showed Socialist films about the persecution of nineteenth-century revolutionaries by the Tsarist regime—there were no Communist films yet; and some emaciated singers sang arias from Mozart and Rossini. These are my childish memories. We all lived in one small room because there was no way to heat more than one. But I was not frightened, and felt no sense of oppression—perhaps I was too young to know what was going on, and my parents seldom spoke of it.

R. J.   How did you arrive in England?

I. B.   We went first to the country, then moved to London. I went to a preparatory school, first in the suburbs of London; at that time I spoke little English, but my parents spoke English to each other. We didn't meet many Russians then or later. My parents felt no nostalgia for Riga or

---

3. Latvia declared its independence in November 1918; recognized by the Soviet Union on 11 August 1920 (Treaty of Riga).

Russia. My father was a fanatical Anglophile—and I grew up in the belief that the English could do no wrong. I preserved my Russian, mainly, I think, by reading the Russian classics. As a result, I speak Russian freely; and on my visits to the Soviet Union I was at times taken for a native. There was one boy in my school who was Russian—his name is Bilibin. His father was a famous Russian painter. His son is still a dedicated Russian monarchist. I did occasionally speak Russian to him, but I met few Russian speakers and my Russian is due mainly to reading and something ingrained in childhood.

OXFORD IN THE 1930s

R. J.   Later you received a scholarship to study at Oxford. Can you tell me what were the main intellectual currents at that time at Oxford?

I. B.   I do not quite know what you mean by "intellectual currents". I do not think that one can identify currents of this sort—in effect philosophies of life, dominant ideas, criss-crossing with other ideas, as happened in continental and certainly Russian universities before the Revolution. I do not think that *animateurs des idées* are a typical English phenomenon. But I may be wrong. I simply did not come across such intellectuals interested in general ideas or passionate advocates of political or social or aesthetic ideas with followers and opponents in Oxford. I did meet people like that after I left the university.

R. J.   There aren't any?

I. B.   Well, of course, I may be exaggerating. They exist. While I was a student in the 1930s there were Socialists, Liberals, Conservatives; the Master of Balliol, A. D.

Lindsay, was a prominent Christian Socialist; there was Douglas Cole who exercised a good deal of influence on undergraduates; there was A. L. Rowse (in those days a Socialist), and a little later Richard Crossman, A. J. P. Taylor, Patrick Gordon Walker. But it is difficult to describe this as a powerful intellectual current. There were young poets, a lot of writing. I edited an intellectual periodical called *The Oxford Outlook*, which two or so years before was edited by the poet Wystan Auden. We read Auden, Spender, Day Lewis, MacNeice. I was a contemporary of Stephen Spender, he is one of my greatest friends, I have known him all my life. He wrote beautiful poetry while he was still a student at Oxford. Most undergraduates of my day were unpolitical. Later there were, of course, radicals and Communists—like my friends N. O. Brown, Philip Toynbee and so on; but nothing like, let us say, post-war Paris, where there was a Merleau-Ponty, or a Sartre. We were liberal-minded; we hated Mussolini, Franco and (some of us) Stalin, and of course Hitler and all the minor dictators then arising in south-eastern Europe. What was going on in France at the time that I was a student? Were Barbusse, Romain Rolland, Gide, politically influential? I do not wish to convey the idea that we were, either when I was a student or in the years before the war when I began to teach, politically passive. My friends and I were anti-Fascist, packed parcels for the supporters of the Spanish Republican Government. But I cannot say that I had pronounced political views apart from general support of liberal movements and progressive forces. There was the Labour Club, which some of us occasionally went to. In the mid-thirties there was a weekly lunch organized by Douglas Cole, which, as I remember, was attended by Crossman, Gordon Walker, Pakenham, Rowse, the philosophers A. J. Ayer, J. L. Austin, Stuart Hampshire, the eminent Roman historian Hugo Jones, Christopher Hill (whom I did not then know to be a Communist, though I do not think he concealed this), the eminent economists

Roy Harrod and James Meade. Meade was the purest liberal I have ever known—he is still amongst us, I am happy to say, a man of about my age. I always felt that if there was a crisis—a revolution in which I might not be quite clear about what I should do—if I followed him I should avoid perpetrating anything squalid or contemptible and would be, if not politically secure, certainly morally safe.

R. J.   Well, Bergsonian philosophy had a great influence at that time in France.

I. B.   There was no philosopher in England who exercised a general influence on the public in the way that Bergson did in France, or Croce in Italy. There were no philosophers whose lectures were attended by fashionable ladies. I was told that in Paris their servants used to come to the lectures in the hall in which Bergson spoke; they came an hour before and attended the lecture of, let us say, some Professor of Assyrian archaeology; he and others were very surprised to find the entire lecture hall so full of odd-looking people very unlike academics. No sooner was the lecture over than the audience rose to its feet and made room for the smart ladies who crowded in to hear Professor Bergson. There has been nothing like this in England since the lectures of Thomas Carlyle.

R. J.   So there was not a great deal of political activity in Oxford at that time?

I. B.   No doubt there was—there was a Socialist and a Communist Club, and the preoccupation with aesthetic values gave place to political interests. The breaking-point in Oxford, I should say, was the financial crisis of 1931. That struck a blow at the prevalent aestheticism which socially had counted a good deal in the Oxford of the 1920s. Harold

Acton, Cyril Connolly, Evelyn Waugh, Brian Howard, were typical "aesthetes", as they were called. There is, indeed, a French book on the subject by Monsieur Jean Fayard called *Margaret et Oxford*—not widely read now, I daresay. The vast majority of these aesthetes are lost to history. To flout academic conventions and to hope to survive in the outer world needed some degree of financial security—that is, support from parents or guardians. The crisis of 1931 hit the affluent quite hard, and this support became precarious henceforth. After this aestheticism declined and left-wing politics came to the fore. Still, I do not think it was anything like the ferment in Paris or before Hitler in the Weimar Republic. Still, the *Zeitgeist* reached me too. I wrote a book on Karl Marx, which to my surprise is still obtainable.

R. J.   Do you consider your interest in the history of ideas was profoundly influenced by your political and philosophical experiences at Oxford?

I. B.   Not exactly. First of all, I couldn't help being affected by the existence of the Soviet Union. I was never attracted by Marxism, nor by the Soviet regime, even though my parents had not been persecuted by it and came to England without in any way being compelled to do so. But I did have memories of the Soviet regime, which were not happy: one or two people we had known who were shot quite early in 1918, not for political reasons. There was no explanation of this from any source. There were a great many executions—there was a terror, nothing like what it grew to be in Stalin's reign, but still, a good many people were shot for reasons that were never revealed to the public except in general terms—"enemies of the Soviet Union", "speculators", "counter-revolutionaries", "supporters of the bourgeoisie", and the like.

9

KARL MARX: MY FIRST COMMISSION

R. J.   Was any member of your family executed?

I. B.   No. None of our relations were executed or even
arrested. My family, as I have already said, was not touched,
the terror was all around us but did not reach us—we went on
holidays in the summer, in a perfectly normal fashion; we did
not starve, we had just enough food and fuel to continue. I
had no sense of horror, but I did, even as a child, have a vague
awareness of a collapse of a society, though not of the
rise of another, new one. My parents were happy only during
the months of February to October 1917, when there was no
censorship, lots of newspapers, endless meetings, oratory,
general exhilaration. In 1918 all this was changed. I sensed that
there was some awareness among the older members of my
family of political ideas as an important factor in human
history. Perhaps those who went to school during the Soviet
period felt it more, but I was taught at home. Still, as a result
of this sense of the circulation of political ideas, notions like
equality, liberalism, socialism, began to mean something to
me quite early in my life. It did not mean much to some of my
contemporaries at school or at university. The aesthetes—
Cyril Connolly, Bernard Spencer, Louis MacNeice and the
like—did not, I believe, think in these terms while they were
students, nor much, I think, later in their lives. Auden and
Spender and Day Lewis did, of course.

But there was another event which had an effect on me.
Mr H. A. L. Fisher, an eminent historian and head of an
Oxford College, was an editor of the Home University
Library—a series of popular books for ordinary readers. In
1933 Fisher asked me to write a book on Karl Marx for this
series. I was very surprised by this offer because I had shown
no signs of interest in the subject, although I did take an
interest in general ideas as well as philosophical ones. Even in
1933 I enjoyed talking to people about social, political,

literary, artistic ideas, but I had no particular interest in Karl Marx. The book was first offered to Harold Laski, who refused. Then it was offered to Frank Pakenham, now Lord Longford, and he, too, refused. Then it was offered to Richard Crossman, and probably to others, who all refused. Finally Fisher offered it to me, and I thought that, well, Marxism was obviously going to be more important and influential, not less. I had read a certain amount of Marx, but not much. *Das Kapital* was a set book for the examination which I took in my fourth year, in addition to Adam Smith and Ricardo—but I found it hard going. Still, I wanted to know what Marx taught—why his following was growing everywhere. I thought that if I never wrote about him I would never read him, because when I read *Das Kapital* I frequently, particularly at the beginning, found it unreadable (as Keynes did, but not perhaps for the same reasons). So I forced myself to read Karl Marx extensively. My German is not too bad, so I read it partly in German, partly in English, partly in Russian, because the authoritative edition of the works of Marx and Engels had been banned by Hitler in 1933 but continued to appear in Moscow, in Russian.

R. J.   I think it was Bakunin who translated *Das Kapital* for the first time into Russian.

I. B.   Well, he began it, but didn't finish it. There was a tremendous row about that—Marx began to suspect Bakunin of all kinds of chicanery. The first complete Russian translation of *Das Kapital*, certainly of Volume I, was made by a professor of economics in the University of Kiev; the Russian Tsarist censorship passed it because the censor thought that it was so abstruse that nobody much would read it.

R. J.   When you began had you already read Lenin and Trotsky?

I. B.   No, not then, but I did later when I started working on Marx and Marxism. Then I began reading Marx's forerunners, the *Encyclopédistes*. I read Helvétius, Holbach, Diderot. I already knew Rousseau quite well. Then I began reading the so-called "Utopian" Socialists—Saint-Simon, Fourier, Owen, and was fascinated by some of their doctrines and arguments, and I looked at Rodbertus, Louis Blanc, Moses Hess. After that, Plekhanov[4], a really brilliant Russian Marxist writer. I read him with complete fascination because he is polemical, witty and wonderfully readable, as well as highly informative and always rational and clear. That gave me the taste for reading Marxist writers, much more, I am afraid, than reading Marx himself in bulk. I read Engels, who of course is a much clearer, if shallower, writer than Marx. I still read Plekhanov with pleasure. He was the man who was, as you know, the true father of Russian Marxism, greatly influenced Lenin and then bitterly quarrelled with him. I read these people and began to lecture on them. In this way I began to work on a subject that had virtually nothing to do with what I taught my students. Nobody in Oxford seemed to have the faintest interest in French eighteenth-century thought. But because I gave lectures on it people started to become interested. I was a member of the wonderful London Library, a private collection, where I found a lot of Russian books which one of the old librarians who was a Slavic scholar had carefully collected. There I found a book by someone I had only vaguely heard of, Alexander Herzen. I read somewhere that he had known Turgenev and Bakunin. Herzen became my

---

4. Georgii Plekhanov (1856–1918) in his youth belonged to the moderate wing of the Populists or *Narodniki* (from the Russian "narod"—"people"). His most notable works include *An Essay on the Development of the Monist Conception of History*, 1895, and *History of Russian Social Thought*. In 1900 in Geneva he founded, with Lenin, the journal *Iskra* (*The Spark*). Returning to Russia after the Revolution of February 1917, he opposed the Bolshevik seizure of power.

hero for the rest of my life. He is a wonderful writer and an acute and honest political thinker, and exceedingly original. His autobiography is perhaps the best I have ever read in my life, even better than Rousseau's. It was Herzen who gave me a real taste for the history of social and political ideas. That is what truly started me off.

THE VIENNA CIRCLE

R. J.   What was your attitude towards the kind of philosophical activity engaged in at that time by your colleagues in the field of logical Positivism?

I. B.   There were no strict logical Positivists at Oxford apart from Freddie Ayer. He began it. He went to Vienna, attended lectures and seminars of the Vienna School, and in 1936 published his famous book *Language, Truth and Logic*, which is a kind of manifesto of this movement. It was written in beautiful English, clear, incisive and highly readable even by those who were not professional philosophers. The dominant philosophy in Oxford before the war was a kind of philosophical realism, directed mainly against Hegel and Idealism—inspired by the British Empiricists, and, of course, G. E. Moore and Bertrand Russell. Plato and Aristotle were of course also studied by those who read Greek, but were, perhaps, rather less influential. The idea that the 1930s were dominated by logical Positivism is not accurate—groups met in London and elsewhere: but the domination came later. I think the main cause of this was Ayer's book. Maybe my friend Ayer, who was my contemporary at Oxford, may have thought that because he had himself been completely absorbed by it, and was certainly the first and most vigorous apostle of logical Positivism in England, that it was more universally dominant among English philosophers than in fact it was. But the influence was very considerable. The source of logical Positivism was

Vienna. In Cambridge there were revisionist Positivists because Wittgenstein was there, and Frank Ramsey, and Braithwaite, and their disciples. The influence of the earlier writings of both Russell and Moore cannot be ignored. In Oxford, even after the war, Positivism had to struggle against something that was called "Oxford philosophy", a kind of general undoctrinaire empiricism, united with an analysis of language. This movement was sometimes called radical empiricism or linguistic analysis. It is a part of an old English tradition, which ultimately derives from Locke, Berkeley, Hume, Mill, Moore and Russell. Russell was not a logical Positivist, though this movement certainly sprang in part from his pioneering work.

R. J.   Well, I talked about it because you wrote about it, didn't you?

I. B.   Yes, of course. I did write about it, because I took an interest in it. But I thought that logical Positivists were in important respects mistaken—some of them were exceedingly fanatical.

R. J.   Do you still think so?

I. B.   Yes. But you know, there are no true logical Positivists left, as far as I know. They did, as I said, have a powerful effect. Schlick, Carnap, Waismann, had an influence on leading English philosophers like Ryle, Wisdom and, at Harvard, Quine, and their pupils.

R. J.   Quine seems to have a lot of influence in the United States?

I. B.   Yes, indeed. I suspect that today the most influential philosopher in the U.S. is probably Donald Davidson. And to a degree a younger man, Saul Kripke.

14

AKHMATOVA AND PASTERNAK

R. J.   During the Second World War you worked for the Foreign Office in Washington and Moscow. Was the change in surroundings from Oxford to the horrors of world war too difficult for you?

I. B.   There were no horrors in Washington—it was shamefully comfortable and most interesting. I was one of a great body of British officials, some of whom, like myself, felt genuinely ashamed of our security while terrible sufferings were being inflicted on our countrymen and others in Europe and elsewhere.

R. J.   How about in Moscow?

I. B.   That was a sudden transition. I began working in New York in 1941 as a British information officer, then I was moved to the British Embassy in Washington as a reporter on American opinion. That was completely different from anything I had done before. The work was not very exacting: one week's work in an embassy—that is my experience—was less of a strain than one day's teaching at Oxford—less interesting, but immeasurably less exhausting. I preferred philosophy to diplomacy. From Washington I went to Moscow in 1945 after Potsdam. I arrived in mid-September and left in January 1946. I was told that I would not meet anybody of interest—only officials who would reveal nothing about anything; but in fact I met writers—especially Pasternak and Akhmatova, both poets of genius, and a good many other writers. I used to visit Pasternak once a week—it was a unique and wonderful experience. I met Akhmatova then only twice, but that was one of the most—perhaps the most—memorable experiences of my life. I have described it all, as best I could, in an essay published in

15

Personal Impressions, so I won't go on about this now[5]. Some of the writers in Russia were heroic and morally deeply impressive people: living and working in intolerable conditions. No one who has not lived in Stalin's Russia can imagine what it was like.

R. J.   There were no problems with Stalin's secret police?

I. B.   Of course there were. My visits did not do some of my acquaintances any good. I think the persecution of Akhmatova was not exactly alleviated by my visits. She told me that Stalin was personally infuriated by the fact that I had met her, and said, "I see that our nun (as he called her) now receives foreign spies." All members of foreign embassies were, of course, considered spies by Stalin and his entourage. Akhmatova had literally not met any foreigner since 1917, save one Pole, which doesn't quite count—nobody from the West, until I called upon her. Of course this moved her. She knew very little of the outside world—and I was able to tell her a good deal, and answer a very great many of her questions. She was not allowed to publish much during Stalin's years[6]. She is a great poet and a genius even as a human being. To know her was one of the greatest privileges and most moving experiences in my life.

R. J.   And how did you find the Soviet Union after so many years?

I. B.   I lived in a building that belonged to the British Embassy. In Moscow at that time foreign embassies were like a zoological gardens—the cages inter-communicated but you couldn't go outside the fence. Perhaps it was differ-

5. In the very beautiful "Poem without a Hero" by Akhmatova Isaiah Berlin appears as "the Guest of the Future".
6. "Half nun, half harlot," as she was so grossly described by Zhdanov, the official party ideologue, in 1948. Akhmatova died in Moscow in 1966 at the age of 77.

ent for representatives of Eastern European countries, at least some of them. But 1945 was a very fortunate year for me, because after Potsdam nobody quite knew who was friend, who was foe. Everything was somewhat confused. Russian intellectuals lived in a kind of false paradise, they met foreigners more easily in the autumn of 1945 than even after Stalin's death. It is a paradox: by 1947–8 all the doors were shut, but in 1945 there was a lot of excitement. Russians came back from Germany and brought stories about the West, and had met people there very unlike those who they had known during previous decades. Russia was a prison— but there seemed new hope now. The last chapters of *Doctor Zhivago* are some indication of the false dawn in which people lived at that time.

R. J.   Have you returned to the Soviet Union since January 1946?

I. B.   Yes. I went back there in 1956 and stayed as a guest of two ambassadors who were friends of mine. I met Pasternak again. By then it was not safe for Russians to talk to foreigners. In 1945 it was not less unsafe, but some of them didn't realize it.

R. J.   Was Pasternak very isolated at that time?

I. B.   You could see Pasternak, because that was before his disgrace, that is, before *Doctor Zhivago* and the Nobel Prize. He gave me the second typescript copy of his book—the first copy was already in the hands of the publisher Feltrinelli in Italy. I read it through in one night, and thought it marvellous. I gave my copy to Pasternak's two sisters, who lived in Oxford.

R. J.   Do you consider Pasternak a great poet or a great novelist?

I. B.   He is of course a great poet. Let me tell you, there are two kinds of poets. There are poets who are poets when they write poetry and prose writers when they write prose, like Pushkin. And there are poets who when they write poetry write poetry, and when they write prose also write poetry. Pasternak belongs to the second category. His prose is always poetical prose, he is not by nature a prose writer in my opinion. He is a great poet, one of the last great Russian poets, and his novel is a great poetical work, one of the few that describe love, the love of the hero for the heroine, describe it genuinely, as few writers—despite the fact that it is the centre of so much fiction—have succeeded in doing. But it is his poetry that accounts for the almost universal admiration which Russians and others who read Russian feel for him. Only Joseph Brodsky comes anywhere near; actually Akhmatova and Mandelshtam mean far more to him. He is, in my opinion (and I am not alone in this), the best living Russian poet anywhere. But not every genius is like one's image of a genius. Pasternak was such a one. He talked marvellously, he was a little unhinged at times, but at all times a man of pure genius. Nobody could have had a more fascinating experience than to listen to him talk—in my experience only Virginia Woolf talked somewhat like that. She, too, of course, was a trifle crazy.

R. J.   In what way?

I. B.   Images, similes, descriptions, wonderful creative, unforgettable language of unbelievable vitality—in the case both of Pasternak and of Mrs Woolf, it made one's thoughts race in one's head. Akhmatova's magic was of a different, but no less powerful, kind.

R. J.   How about Mayakovsky and Esenin?

I. B.   I did not know them.

R. J.   But what is your impression when you read their poems?

I. B.   Mayakovsky also was a kind of genius. He was an important poet because he altered the way in which poetry was written in Russia. He was a pioneer of a very dominant kind. There are certain people who without necessarily being great poets—and I cannot think that Mayakovsky was a truly great poet, but many critics disagree with me—are great "animateurs", rather like Ezra Pound, who certainly changed the way in which English poetry is written; whether he is a great poet is equally questionable, but there is no doubt about his impact on poetry, and that certainly is a form of artistic genius. Mayakovsky was like that: he was a tremendous orator, a bold innovator, a genuine revolutionary, but his poetry doesn't speak to me as Pasternak's or Mandelshtam's or Akhmatova's does.

DISCOVERY OF AUSCHWITZ

R. J.   How did you experience the Second World War as a Jew?

I. B.   I do not think that my reactions were different from those of the vast majority of Jews outside the area controlled by the Germans and Italians. Horror about what was happening was appalling and continuous. But other people must have felt it too. There is something in this connection which I must confess with a degree of shame. I assumed from the very beginning that Hitler meant to inflict terrible sufferings on the Jews—he was a fiend and implacable, that was obvious. We all knew that Jews had been imprisoned, and some were killed, in concentration camps, from 1933 onwards. And this was not publicized sufficiently in the West. And the efforts to control immigration by refugees were shameful—France behaved decently in comparison, for example, with the United States, in this respect. After the invasion of Poland, I assumed that terrible things were happening to Jews, that they would be arrested, persecuted, tortured, perhaps killed, but none of us knew what was going on. Before the events of the Warsaw ghetto, no news came. We just assumed appalling horrors. Before 1944 I knew nothing about systematic extermination—the gas chambers. Nobody told me, in England or America; there was nothing about it in anything I read—perhaps that was my own fault. That makes me feel ashamed. There probably were articles on back pages or news items in newspapers, but I missed them. The first time the full news of the horrors came out was when someone came and reported this in Switzerland. There was a man who got the news to a Rabbi in New York, who went to see President Roosevelt; but nothing was done and nothing was made public. At any rate I continued to know nothing of it. I think that my wife's family who were French Jews, knew something by 1942–3 —perhaps they did not believe it—few people could bring themselves to believe that something like this could be happening, many dismissed it as exaggerated. I never heard about this until the end of 1944. Even by 1943–4 I realized that the Nazis wanted to kill Jews even more than they wanted to win the war—the killing went on steadily when Germany was plainly heading for defeat in 1945. But, as I said before, I only discovered the full horror of the holocaust very late. I do not know why nobody ever told me— perhaps life in an embassy was too protected. Still, I met prominent American Jews from time to time, and nobody ever told me about this. I still feel some guilt about it, even though it was not really any fault of mine.

R. J. Were any members of your family killed by the Nazis?

I. B.   Yes. Both my grandfathers, an uncle, an aunt, three cousins, were killed in Riga in 1941.

R. J.   What was your reaction once you knew about the extermination of the Jews? I ask you this question because you haven't written on this subject.

I. B.   I felt exactly like everybody else. I thought that it was the greatest disaster that had ever happened to the Jews, worse than the destruction of the second Temple. What can one possibly say about so great a horror? I didn't change my opinions. I thought that the one thing it proved historically was that Marx and Hegel proved false prophets—that and the hopelessness of assimilation. Nobody was more deeply assimilated than the German Jews. German Jews were, and perhaps some still are, more German than the Germans— French Jews were deeply French and remained so, but the fact is that even these people had no inkling that something like this could happen. There were memories of pogroms in Eastern Europe or North Africa, but these seemed remote by 1939. German Jews could, I am sure, not conceive of such a possibility—their German patriotism was too deeply ingrained. Let me tell you a characteristic story: I met a German Jew once in London, in 1946. He told me that he left Germany in 1933 and that he then went to live in Switzerland. I asked him why he didn't go to Paris, which was surely more interesting—he was a lively man, much interested in literature and the theatre. He said "I would never dream of going to a country of our enemies". You cannot deny that a man who says this cannot be (subjectively) more German than that. I don't wish to generalize—many Jews did go to Paris, after all, and were duly killed later in German camps.

R. J.   Walter Benjamin was one of these?

21

I. B.   He committed suicide on the Spanish frontier. But others were taken to Auschwitz or Belsen from France, from a camp in Drancy. People used to ask why the Allies did not bomb the German trains carrying people to the camps. I never thought that it would have done any good, because I feel sure to this day that the Nazis were so terribly intent on killing Jews that even if the trains had been bombed, or indeed the camps too, they would have been rebuilt immediately. They hated the Jews, I feel convinced, more than they feared losing the war. The one thing which they would never have allowed to stop were the trains of the doomed and the gas chambers. I think that some Jews could have been saved in other Eastern European countries, the Balkans, etc., if the Allies had threatened these countries violently enough with vengeance if the Jews were handed over to the Germans—particularly when it was no longer certain, say by 1943, that the Germans would inevitably win the war—there was plenty of anti-Semitism in these countries, of course, as there still is, but it is not of the pathologically fanatical kind which characterized the Nazis, and fear of punishment might have had some effect among these peoples. I do not know why this was not sufficiently done.

R. J.   Later, in 1957, you received a knighthood. From 1957–67 you taught social and political theory at Oxford. From 1966–75 you were the first President of Wolfson College, Oxford. Later you were elected President of the British Academy, 1974–8. Did you have to perform many journeys on behalf of the Academy?

I. B.   I went to Iran in 1977 to open the building at the British School of Archaeology in Teheran on behalf of the British Academy. The Shah was still on the throne.

R. J.   Was this the first time you had travelled in the East?

I. B.   No, I had already been to India. I spent a few days in Teheran on my way back from India in the early 1970s.

R. J.   And what was your impression of the East?

I. B.   "The East" covers too vast a territory. In Iran my wife and I went to Shiraz and Isfahan. I remember a student who walked up to me outside the great mosque with the wonderful blue dome in Isfahan and asked "Is there anything in England as great and as beautiful as this?" I thought, and in the end said "I don't think so." I went to Mashad. The processions round the Imam's tomb by men who seemed to me to wear fanatical expressions on their faces terrified me. I had never seen anything so frightening since the Russian Revolution.

PHILOSOPHER OR HISTORIAN OF IDEAS?

R. J.   In many of your essays you try to show the emergence of ideas by bringing them to light through the life and personality of their authors. Do you consider your work a philosophical investigation or an historical one?

I. B.   How can I distinguish? Let me explain: take, for example, the history of philosophy. Some histories of philosophy throw little light on it because, unless the writer is or has been a student of philosophy himself, unless he has thought about philosophical problems as such, he cannot have any idea of what it is that made someone else think these thoughts or be tormented by these problems. He cannot truly grasp what questions philosophers have attempted to answer or analyse or discuss. He will simply transcribe—he will write that Descartes said this, Spinoza said that, but that Hume did not think that either was right. That is all quite dead. Unless you have yourself spent sleepless nights about philosophical problems, you cannot possibly tell that there exists such a subject. What philosophy is, is itself a philosophical question, to which ordinary people do not have clear answers. To write a good illuminating history of philosophy you must try to see these problems from the "inside", so far as you can. You must try and enter imaginatively into the mental world of the philosophers you are discussing. You must try to enter into what the ideas meant to those who entertained them, what were the kinds of things that were central to them. Without that there can be no true history of ideas. My interest was not centred on mainly philosophical ideas, but also on social, political and artistic ideas. Again, unless you are yourself involved in such topics and are puzzled by such problems, you cannot write a significant history of the similar preoccupations of others. The history of ideological positions cannot be written properly except by those who are themselves liable to think in ideological terms, and are aware that they are doing so.

R. J.   What do you mean by ideology in this sense?

I. B.   In the sense that these ideas must make a difference to you. An intellectual is a person who wants ideas to be as interesting as possible. Unless you think the ideas you are discussing are interesting to you, whatever you may believe yourself, the history of ideas will remain a mechanical catalogue of unexamined doctrines, terribly boring and unreal. I am interested in certain ideas. If you are interested in ideas and they matter to you, you cannot but be interested in the history of these ideas, because ideas are not monads, they are not born in the void, they relate to other ideas, beliefs, forms of life, outlooks—outlooks, *Weltanschauungen*, flow out of one another and are part of what is called "the intellectual climate", and form people and their actions and their feelings as much as material factors and historical change.

R. J.   I asked this question because I remembered that in your article "Nationalism" you consider yourself neither a historian, nor a political scientist. Therefore I thought maybe you think of yourself as a philosopher.

I. B.   My view of philosophy is coloured by my fascination with the genesis and development of general ideas. Let me explain what I mean. There are certain subjects which advance by accumulation: that is progress. If you are a chemist you don't need to study Lavoisier unless you are interested in the history of chemistry. If you are a chemist today you have to know what chemists are thinking today. And this is true for all subjects which progress, inasmuch as we can affirm that we know more today than we knew yesterday. Philosophy is not like that. It does not advance in that sense. You do not say "Plato said this, Aristotle said that, but we have gone far beyond them, so there is no need to read them—they are as obsolete as Archimedes or Roger Bacon—or if not obsolete at any rate totally superseded". The questions Plato asked can still be, and indeed are, asked today. The questions which Herder and Vico asked are still debated. Aristotle is a direct influence on present-day philosophers, not only on Thomas Aquinas. Philosophy is not a cumulative discipline. The major ideas, outlooks, theories, insights, have remained the central ideas of philosophy. They have a certain life of their own which is trans-historical. Some people disagree. They say you can only understand questions and ideas in terms of the historical environment in which they occur. How can you understand Machiavelli without accurate knowledge of events in Florence, life in Italy, in the fifteenth century? How can you understand Spinoza if you know nothing about Holland or France in the

25

seventeenth? There is some truth in that, but only some. Historians who have never been philosophers say that people who take an interest in Machiavelli must absorb themselves in the Renaissance. No doubt this helps. If you understand the circumstances of the questions he was asking, and why they occupied his thoughts, you will certainly understand him better. I don't mean that the *mentalités* discussed in *Annales* are not important. They are. Let me ask you: how much do we know about Athens—the *mentalité*, or the ways of life, in the days of Socrates or Plato or Xenophon? We scarcely know what Athens looked like—did it look like Beirut or like a Zulu kraal? The Parthenon, the other temples—yes, of course; and there are remains of dwellings. But we do not know what the streets really looked like, what kind of food they liked, what their speech sounded like, what they looked like—despite the vase paintings and the statues—we don't know the details of family life, of the relations of free men to slaves, of the rich to the poor; we try to construct ideas about these things, but in comparison with what we know about more recent centuries, we are certainly ignorant. And yet Plato's ideas mean something, indeed, a great deal to us today, even without the environmental knowledge that ideally is needed to understand what Greek words mean. Central ideas, the great ideas which have occupied minds in the Western world, have a certain life of their own—we may not understand precisely what they meant to Athenians, we may not know how Greek or Latin were pronounced, we may not understand inflexions, nuances, references, allusions—but major ideas survive in some sense despite the ignorance of the material aspects or historical details of the world in which they were born and exercised influence. But of course there are a good many ideas, political, social, moral, which perish with the societies in which they lived—which can only be studied historically with an imperfect understanding of how they came to be so powerful and so influential.

PHILOSOPHY WITHOUT PHILOSOPHERS?

R. J.   But you do believe that philosophy is an eternal question?

I. B.   Certainly. Philosophy comes from the collision of ideas which create problems. The ideas come from life. Life changes, so do the ideas, so do the collisions. The collisions breed puzzles, but when life changes these puzzles are not so much answered as die away. Ideas perish from inanition far more frequently than as a result of being refuted by argument. Because of this, and the social changes that breed new problems, the very idea that you can even in principle find solutions to all questions, is absurd. You cannot, because philosophy is not like inorganic chemistry, where perhaps you really can answer all the questions—but I suspect even there you cannot. Philosophy has to do with puzzles which arise from some kind of conflict of words or ideas or ways of speech in which they are expressed. Problems arise because an attempted solution to a problem is not compatible with methods of solving another kind of problem. Philosophical questions are not like empirical problems, which can be answered by observation or experiment or entailments from them. Nor are they like mathematical problems which can be settled by deductive methods, like problems in chess or any other rule-governed game or procedure. But questions about the ends of life, about good and evil, about freedom and necessity, about objectivity and relativity, cannot be decided by looking into even the most sophisticated dictionary or the use of empirical or mathematical reasoning. Not to know where to look for the answer is the surest symptom of a philosophical problem. Fermat's Theorem has not been solved, but the methods of treating it are not in doubt: one knows what a proof—if it is found—would look like. Not so with philosophy. The history of ideas is a very different matter. There we really do try and trace the development of ideas. The history of ideas is the history of what we believe that people thought and felt, and these people were real people, not just statues or collections of attributes. Some effort to enter imaginatively into the minds and outlooks of the thinkers of the thoughts is indispensable, an effort at *Einfühlung* is unavoidable, however precarious and difficult and uncertain. When I was working on Marx, I tried to understand what it was like to be Karl Marx in Berlin, in Paris, in Brussels, in London, and to think in terms of his concepts, categories, his German words. It was the same thing with Vico and Herder, Herzen, Tolstoy, Sorel, whoever. How were their ideas born? In what particular time, place, society? Their ideas may be interesting as such, but they are their ideas, and you must ask yourself what bothered them, what made them torment themselves over these issues. How did their theories or writings mature in their heads? One cannot talk about ideas in complete abstraction, unhistorically; but neither can one talk solely in terms of concrete historical milieux, as if ideas made no sense outside their frameworks. As you can see, this is a complex, imprecise, psychologically demanding, imagination-requiring field of enquiry, in which nothing like certainty can ever be obtained, only, at the most, a high degree of plausibility and coherence and evidence of intellectual power and originality and effectiveness.

R. J.   Do you think philosophy can survive without philosophers?

I. B.   It depends what you call philosophers. Ordinary men with sufficient curiosity and capacity for understanding general ideas can, of course, philosophize. Herzen, for example, was not a professional philosopher, nor were Marx or Dostoevsky, yet their ideas still have considerable philosophical importance. It depends on what you mean. Bodin was a lawyer. So was Bacon. They were not professors. Nor were Leibniz or Spinoza or Descartes or Hume. Berkeley was a Bishop. Before Christian Wolff I know of no professional professor of philosophy—perhaps Thomasius was one—Vico certainly was not, he taught rhetoric and law.

R. J.   So you think philosophy can exist outside professional philosophy?

I. B.   Of course. I think that professional philosophers are needed because if they are any good they do clarify ideas; they analyse words and concepts and the ordinary terms in which you and I think, and this makes a great deal of difference to the progress of thought. Perhaps freedom from thought would make us happier, but it is not attainable. Still, it is the basic difference between human beings and animals. Let me tell you a story which is merely an anecdote. The late Harold Macmillan told me that when he was a student at Oxford, before the First World War, he went to the lectures of a philosopher called J. A. Smith, a Hegelian metaphysician. In his first lecture to his audience of students, this professor spoke as follows: "All of you, gentlemen, will have different careers—some of you will be lawyers, some of you will be soldiers, some will be doctors or engineers, some will be government servants, some will be landowners or politicians. Let me tell you at once that nothing I say during these lectures will be of the slightest use to you in any of the fields in which you will attempt to exercise your skills. But one thing I can promise you: if you continue with this course of lectures to the end, you will always be able to know when men are talking rot." There is some validity in that remark. One of the effects of philosophy, if it is properly taught, is ability to see through political rhetoric, bad arguments, deceptions, *fumisme*, verbal fog, emotional blackmail and every kind of chicanery and disguise. It can sharpen the critical faculty a very great deal.

R. J.   So you don't agree with the Hegelian project of philosophy as a science?

I. B.   No. Philosophy consists of trying to move towards resolving problems where *prima facie* there appears to exist no obvious technique for finding the answers. I think Kant is a great philosopher in part because he understood the nature of philosophy in this sense. Moreover, I think that self-understanding is one of the main purposes of philosophy. One of the aims of philosophy is to understand the relationships of men, things, and words to each other.

R. J.   So you feel closer to a philosopher like Schopenhauer than to Hegel?

I. B.   Yes. I do not find all-embracing systems, vast metaphysical edifices congenial. One can ignore Schopenhauer's system, yet derive great profit from his many sharp and sometimes profound insights. The Hegelian system seems to me a dark, deep cave of Polyphemus, from which few return—all the footsteps point one way, as the Latin poet pointed out.

R. J.   In most of your writings you are more concerned with post-Renaissance thinkers than with the Greek and Roman classical thinkers. As a result, you seem voluntarily to distance yourself from the tradition of political philosophy which stays critical towards modernity. Is this your intention?

I. B.   Who exactly are the Roman thinkers?

R. J.   Well, Cicero, Seneca.

I. B.   Who, to your knowledge, writes about Roman thought from a philosophical point of view? Who today has been influenced by Seneca or even Cicero? Can you give me the names of any of their modern disciples? Seneca's plays have played their part in European literature, and Roman Stoicism in social and educational and perhaps political history. But philosophical influence? Rome was not a very philosophical nation. The Greeks are another matter. We are all in the deepest debt to them.

THE "MAGIC EYE" OF LEO STRAUSS

R. J.   What do you think about Leo Strauss and his political philosophy?

I. B.   I knew Leo Strauss personally and liked him. He was a very learned man, a genuine classical and Talmudic scholar, who thought that political philosophy went gravely wrong with Machiavelli—"the teacher of evil"—and has never recovered since. For him, no political thinker since the Middle Ages had found the true path. Burke came nearest to it, but Hobbes and his followers had gone badly wrong and gravely misled others. Utilitarianism, empiricism, relativism, subjectivism—these were the profound fallacies which had deeply perverted modern thought and had done grave damage to individuals and societies. Objective Good and Evil, Right and Wrong, have been dethroned. Strauss was a careful, honest and deeply concerned thinker, who seemed to have taught his pupils to read between the lines of the classical philosophers—he had a theory that these thinkers had secret doctrines beneath the overt one—which could only be discovered by hints, allusions and other symptoms, sometimes because such thinkers thought in this fashion, sometimes for fear of censorship, oppressive regimes and the like. This has been a great stimulus to ingenuity and all kinds of fanciful subtleties, but seems to me to be wrongheaded. Strauss's rejection of the post-Renaissance world as hopelessly corrupted by Positivism and empiricism seems to me to border on the absurd.

R. J.   How about his critique of modernity?

I. B.   I have little sympathy with it. He did try to convert me in many conversations when I was a visitor in Chicago, but he could not get me to believe in eternal, immutable, absolute values, true for all men everywhere at all times, God-given Natural Law and the like. I gather that in one of his essays to be published soon—a posthumous work which had lain unread for some years—I am about to be severely attacked. So be it. I cannot answer him, for he is in his grave, and I have too little interest in his many disciples. He and they appear to me to believe in absolute good and evil, right and wrong, directly perceived by means of a kind of *a priori* vision, a metaphysical eye—by the use of a Platonic rational faculty which has not been granted to me. Plato, Aristotle, the Bible, the Talmud, Maimonides, perhaps Aquinas, and other Scholastics of the Middle Ages, knew what was the best life for men. So did he, and his disciples claim this today. I am not so privileged.

R. J.   So you consider yourself purely as a modern?

I. B.   I don't know what that means. Empirically-minded, yes. I cannot sum up all my beliefs in two words, but I think that all there is in the world is persons and things and ideas in people's heads—goals, emotions, hopes, fears, choices, imaginative visions and all other forms of human experience. That is all I am acquainted with. But I cannot claim omniscience. Perhaps there is a world of eternal truths, values, which the magic eye of the true thinker can perceive—surely this can only belong to an elite to which I fear I have never been admitted. Leo Strauss is right to think that I disagree with his doctrines in principle. I think his best book is that on Hobbes, which he wrote in England—he told me that he thought it was his least good: so there is an unbridgeable chasm between us.

R. J.   And how do you place your philosophy in the tradition of political philosophy?

I. B.   What do you mean by tradition?

R. J.   I mean the tradition from Plato's to today's world.

I. B.   I do not think there is a single tradition. Plato's is one, Aristotle's is another. Spinoza is profoundly different from either, and Kant from all three. So, for example, Plato, Aristotle and the Christian Middle Ages supposed that everything in the world has a purpose, given it by God or Nature. All things and all creatures seek to fulfil that for which they were created or from which they sprang into being. Spinoza denied this. So did Hume. The French *philosophes* believed it, as did Locke. Kant did not, though he had hopes of a fulfilment beyond the grave. Nor did Bentham. Where is this tradition of which you speak?

R. J.   Even in the realm of political philosophy? Is it then a perpetual creation?

I. B.   Yes, *philosophia perennis* is a Christian and especially Roman Catholic concept. Teleology is only one strand in the continuity of this province of thought.

ON CULTURAL DIFFERENCES

R. J.   Among thinkers of modernity you pay particular attention to Vico and Herder. Is it correct to say that your considerations on history were influenced most by these two thinkers?

I. B.   What you say about Vico and Herder is true, I do not own to many considerations of my own on history. I am not a philosopher of history in the proper sense. I believe in pluralism and do not believe in historical determinism. At crucial moments, at turning points, when factors appear more or less equally balanced, chance, individuals and their decisions and acts, themselves not necessarily predictable—indeed, seldom so—can determine the course of history. I do not believe in a libretto of history (that is a phrase used by Herzen, who did not think that history was a drama with acts—a play with a theme created by God or Nature, a carpet with a recognizable pattern). Marx and Hegel did believe that history was a drama, with successive acts where in the end, after, it may be, great upheavals and, for Marx, terrible conflicts and tribulations and disasters, the gates of Paradise will open, there will be a final dénouement: then history will stop—what Marx calls pre-history—and all things will be forever harmonious and men will act in rational cooperation. Vico and Herder said scarcely anything of that type. They believed in certain patterns, especially Vico, but not in a play with a dénouement. My view comes, I suppose, from reading Hegel, Marx and their followers, and finding their arguments totally unconvincing. I feel the same about other pattern-discoverers—Spengler, Toynbee, and their predecessors from Plato and Polybius onwards. Of course people will always seek for purpose and explanation of history of this type, but it seems to me that the facts do not bear this out, the laws are broken by too many obvious exceptions and counter-examples. I have read enough Braudel, E. H. Carr, and modern Marxists, to know what their arguments are, what historical determinists believe in, and although of course there are great impersonal factors which determine the shapes of the lives of individuals and nations, I see no reason to see history as an autobahn from which major deviations cannot occur. I am interested in Vico's and Herder's beliefs in the plurality of cultures, each

with its own centre of gravity—in a variety of cultures with
different, novel, unpredicted outlooks and conflicting attitudes. Vico seems to me to have understood, as no one
before him, that cultures—the sense of what the world
meant to societies, of men and women's collective sense of
themselves in relation to others and the environment—that
which affects particular forms of thought, feeling,
behaviour, action—that cultures differ. Vico discriminated
this in terms of periods, Herder in terms of various contemporary national civilizations as well as those which arose
at other times. This reinforced my idea that history is not a
rigid, linear progression. Voltaire thought of history as a
kind of continuous progress of reason and knowledge and
the creation of works of art, broken by terrible inter-
ruptions—collapses into barbarism—e.g. the superstitious
Christian Middle Ages. I see no incremental progression. Of
course more knowledge, more happiness, more kindness,
more freedom, more efficiency, represent advances. Of some
of these developments one can say that there are more now
than at some other period: of others, less. Can anybody in
the twentieth century—certainly one of the worst centuries
of human history—really believe in uninterrupted human
progress? Or general progress as such? Without specifying
progress in respect of what, can one speak of progress? One
can speak of a system of values which most men in the West
accept today and did not two thousand years ago; and this is
progressive in terms of our values, in some respects, in others
not. But a general movement—I do not perceive it.

R. J.   But you do apply the principle of causality to history,
don't you?

I. B.   Of course. One cannot not apply it. But what I do
not believe is that you can see a pattern enabling you to
predict, as one does in astronomy or even biology. Some of
Marx's, Saint-Simon's, Burckhardt's predictions came true,

some did not. Saint-Simon predicted technological trans-
formation of society, he was totally wrong about the decay
of politics. Marx predicted big business and the effect of
technological progress on culture, but was totally wrong
about the time, place, causes, results, economic effects of
political revolutions. Who today dares repeat Lenin's pre-
diction of the withering away of the state, or Trotsky's
vision of universal flowering of individual genius among
human beings? What none of these prophets predicted was
the rise of nationalism over the entire globe today, nor that
of religious fanaticism, one of the most powerful factors of
our present world. These phenomena were in the nineteenth
century thought to be on the way out—certainly nationalism, and no one assumed that it existed anywhere but in
the West. Marx thought that religion was a by-product of
the class war and capitalism; he did not predict that, let us
say, the Algerian regime, Socialist in principle, would be far
more fanatically religious and racially conscious than Socialist. Prophecy is not an uncommon, but it is not a dependable,
activity. What I find valuable in Vico and Herder is the very
idea of cultural diversity as intrinsic to human history; that
history does not move in straight lines; that between different cultures there is an interplay, sometimes of a causal kind,
but there is not a single key to the future or the past—no
analogy with the physical sciences, the laws of which do
open doors about causal chains which repeat themselves and
can be summarized in general laws.

R. J.   When you speak of the conflict of goals between
individuals do you base this argument on Vico's thought?

I. B.   Vico teaches us to understand alien cultures, in that
sense he differs from the thinkers of the Middle Ages.
Herder, even more than Vico, discriminated between
Greece, Rome, Judaea, India, the German Middle Ages,
Scandinavia, the Holy Roman Empire, France. The fact that

we are able to understand how people live in the way they do, even if they are different from us, even if they are hateful to us and sometimes condemned by us, means that we can communicate across time and space. When we claim to understand people who have a culture very different from our own, it implies the existence of some power of sympathetic understanding, insight, *Einfühlen*—a word invented by Herder. Even if these cultures repel us, one can, by an effort of empathetic imagination, conceive how it could be possible that men—*nos semblables*—can think these thoughts, feel these feelings, pursue these goals, commit these acts.

CULTURAL RELATIVISM AND THE RIGHTS OF MAN

R. J. Don't you think that there is a contrast between the principle of universality and cultural relativism?

I. B. I don't think so. The differences among peoples and societies can be exaggerated. No culture that we know lacks the notions of good and bad; true and false. Courage, for example, has, so far as we can tell, been admired in every society known to us. There are universal values. This is an empirical fact about mankind, what Leibniz called *vérités du fait*, not *vérités de la raison*. There are values that a great many human beings in the vast majority of places and situations, at almost all times, do in fact hold in common, whether consciously and explicitly or as expressed in their behaviour, gestures, actions. On the other hand, there are great differences. If you succeed, or even think that you have succeeded, in understanding in what way individuals, groups, nations, entire civilizations differ from one another and, by an effort of imagination, "enter" into their thoughts and feelings, imagine how you yourself, placed in their circumstances, could view the world, or view yourself in relation to others; then, even if you are repelled by what you find (*tout com-*

prendre is certainly not *tout pardonner*), this must diminish blind intolerance and fanaticism. Imagination can feed fanaticism, but imaginative insight into situations very different from yours must in the end weaken it. Take the Nazis, a very extreme example: people said that they were mad, pathological cases. This seems to me too glib, too easy, too dismissive. The Nazis were led to believe by those who preached to them by word of mouth or printed words that there existed people, correctly described as sub-human, *Untermenschen*, and that these persons were poisonous creatures, who undermined true, i.e. Germanic or Nordic, culture. The proposition that there are *Untermenschen* is quite simply false, empirically false, demonstrable nonsense. But if you believe it, because someone has told you so, and you trust this persuader, then you arrive at a state of mind where, in a sense quite rationally, you believe it necessary to exterminate Jews—this does not spring from lunacy, nor is it mere irrational hatred or contempt or an aggressive tendency, though no doubt these help; these attributes are common enough as the cause of much conflict and violence throughout human history. No, these emotions are organized by means of belief in monstrous untruths, taught systematically by orators or writers; demonstrably false, but clearly stated, doctrines which issue in crimes which lead to dreadful cruelties and vast destructive catastrophes. I think one must be careful in calling thinking people mad or pathological. Persecution need not be insane: only spring from a conviction of the truth of appallingly false beliefs, which can lead to the most unspeakable consequences. If one wishes to prevent the harm done by fanatics, one must try to understand the intellectual, not merely the psychological, roots of their beliefs; one must try to demonstrate to them that they are wrong. If this fails, then one may have to go to war against them. But the attempt to persuade must always be made. Marxism goes to war too easily and quickly. So do some religious movements. They ignore what is common to men's beliefs. Rational methods, roads to the truth, apart from their value in themselves, are, as Socrates taught, of cardinal importance to the fate of individuals and societies: about that the central traditions of Western philosophy are right. The poet Heine a long time ago said that one should not ignore the humble professor in his study; he has considerable power, which must not be under-estimated; unlike his friend Karl Marx, he believed that Kant led to Robespierre. Understanding oneself and others, rational methods, verification, the basis of our knowledge and of all science, as well as the attempt to check intuitive certainties, are of cardinal importance. The idea of human rights rests on the true belief that there are certain goods—freedom, justice, pursuit of happiness, honesty, love—that are in the interest of all human beings, as such, not as members of this or that nationality, religion, profession, character; and that it is right to meet these claims and to protect people against those who ignore or deny them. There are certain things which human beings require as such, not because they are Frenchmen, Germans or medieval scholars or grocers but because they lead human lives as men and women.

R. J.   But don't you think that these principles could be in contradiction to the spirit of nations?

I. B.   I do not. I think that every culture which has ever existed assumed that there exist such rights—or at least a minimum of them. There may be disagreement about how far to expand this minimum—to helots, slaves, Jews, atheists, enemies, members of neighbouring tribes, barbarians, heretics—but that such rights exist and that they are an empirical pre-condition of the leading of full human lives— that has been recognized by every culture. Denial of humanity to certain classes of human beings sometimes occurs in practice, but less often in theory.

R. J.   So, do you think that we can found a political philosophy on the basis of human rights?

I. B.   No, that is not enough. But it is a *sine qua non*. You can't do without it.

R. J.   What does one need to add?

I. B.   It depends. You have to add an analysis of important concepts. You must have a view of what justice is, what freedom is, what social bonds are; you have to distinguish types of liberty, authority, obligation and the like. Political theories often differ in the way they answer a central question—"Why should anyone obey anyone?"—not why do they obey, but why should they; and how far. Most political theories are answers to this kind of question.

TWO CONCEPTS OF LIBERTY

R. J.   Speaking of liberty, can you explain your distinction between positive liberty and negative liberty?

I. B.   There are two separate questions. One is "How many doors are open to me?"; the other is "Who is in charge here? Who is in control?". These questions are interwoven, but they are not the same, and they require different answers. How many doors are open to me? The question about the extent of negative liberty is to do with what obstacles lie before me. What am I prevented from doing by other people—deliberately or indirectly, unintentionally or institutionally. The other question is "Who governs me? Do others govern me or do I govern myself? If others, by what right, what authority? If I have a right to self-rule, auton-omy, can I lose this right? Can I give it away? Waive it? Recover it? In what way? Who makes the laws? Or implements them? Am I consulted? Does the majority govern? Why? Does God? The priests? The Party? The pressure of public opinion? Of tradition? By what authority?" That is a separate question. Both questions, and their sub-questions, are central and legitimate. Both have to be answered. The only reason for which I have been suspected of defending negative liberty against positive and saying that it is more civilized, is because I do think that the concept of positive liberty, which is of course essential to a decent existence, has been more often abused or perverted than that of negative liberty. Both are genuine questions; both are inescapable. And the answers to them determine the nature of a given society—whether it is liberal or authoritarian, democratic or despotic, secular or theocratic, individualistic or communitarian, and so on. Both these concepts have been politically and morally twisted into their opposites. George Orwell is excellent on this. People say "I express your real wishes. You may think that you know what you want, but I, the Führer, we, the Party Central Committee, know you better than you know yourself, and provide you with what you would ask for if you recognized your 'real' needs". Negative liberty is twisted when I am told that liberty must be equal for the tigers and for the sheep, and that this cannot be avoided even if it enables the former to eat the latter, if coercion by the state is not to be used. Of course unlimited liberty for capitalists destroys the liberty of the workers, unlimited liberty for factory-owners or parents will allow children to be employed in the coal-mines. Certainly the weak must be protected against the strong, and liberty to that extent be curtailed. Negative liberty must be curtailed if positive liberty is to be sufficiently realized; there must be a balance between the two, about which no clear principles can be enunciated. Positive and negative liberty are both perfectly valid concepts, but it seems to me that historically more damage has been done by pseudo-positive than by pseudo-negative liberty in the modern world. That, of course, may be disputed. A thinker whom I greatly admire is Benjamin Constant—his discussion of the two kinds of liberty in his essay called "*De la Liberté des Anciens comparée à celle des Modernes*" is one of the best I know on this topic.

R. J.   Exactly—that was my question. Where do you place yourself in the debate between Constant and Rousseau on the contrast between ancient liberty and modern liberty?

I. B.   I am with Constant. Constant said that there are two kinds of liberty. He didn't deny the value of liberty as conceived in ancient Athens. For the Athenians liberty meant that anybody could bring charges against anybody else before the Assembly; anybody could look through the window into anybody else's room. No one had the right to prevent anyone, however humble, from bringing a case against him or her in the law courts, from denouncing them in public, from observing, criticizing, talking freely, whatever the degree of discomfort this might cause. But the modern conception of liberty allows you a right to a certain measure of privacy. Privacy is not a concept frequent in ancient, or indeed medieval thought. Pascal said that all the ills of the world come from the fact that men do not sit quietly in a room. Modern liberty confers this right.

R. J.   But this is private liberty, not public liberty?

I. B.   Yes. But uncontrolled exercise of either liberty destroys the other. The notion of privacy is indeed new, newer than one might think. New concepts do get born: new ideals arise. Take the notion of sincerity. Sincerity was not, so far as I can tell, considered a virtue in the ancient world or in the Middle Ages. Truth, of course, is a cardinal value; martyrdom is exalted, but only if it is bearing witness to the truth, not to a set of false beliefs, however sincerely held; no Jew or Christian thought that while what pagans believed was indeed false yet one could not but admire the sincerity with which these dangerous fallacies were held. No Crusader ever said that what the Moslems believed was, of course, absurd, but that one was moved by the sincerity of such misplaced devotion. No Catholic ever said during the wars of religion that Protestants were dangerous teachers of evil, who led souls to perdition, poisoners who must be resisted and if need be destroyed, yet the fact that they preached what they preached, not to get money, or power, not out of vanity, but simply because they truly believed it and were ready to die for their terrible heresies—that such sincerity was to be admired. Truth alone mattered, I doubt if the idea of sincerity as a virtue is much earlier than the late seventeenth century. Sincerely held error was all the more dangerous and of no moral or spiritual value—at best to be pitied. So, too, variety as a positive value is a new idea. The old idea is that truth is one, error is many. To any real question, only one true answer can in principle be given; the other answers are necessarily false. The idea that there can be two sides to a question, that there may be two or more incompatible answers, any one of which could be accepted by honest, rational men—that is a very recent notion. Some think that Pericles said something of this kind in his famous Funeral Speech. He comes close to it but does not reach it. If Athenian democracy is good then Sparta or Persia cannot be accepted. The merit of a free society is that it allows of a great variety of conflicting opinions without the need for suppression—that is surely comparatively new in the West.

THE DEBATE ON PLURALISM

R. J.   One of the main philosophical concepts which you discuss in a lot of your writings is the concept of pluralism, which you oppose to monism or faith in a single criterion. Do you formulate this concept just in defence of the old liberal political theory, or do you consider it an important factor in dealing with thinkers like Machiavelli and Montesquieu on the one hand, Turgenev and Herzen on the other?

I. B.   Pluralism and liberalism are not the same or even overlapping concepts. There are liberal theories which are not pluralistic. I believe in both liberalism and pluralism, but they are not logically connected. Pluralism entails that, since it is possible that no final answers can be given to moral and political questions, or indeed any questions about value, and more than that, that some answers that people give, and are entitled to give, are not compatible with each other, room must be made for a life in which some values may turn out to be incompatible, so that if destructive conflict is to be avoided compromises have to be effected, and a minimum degree of toleration, however reluctant, becomes indispensable.

R. J.   Do you consider Machiavelli a pluralistic thinker?

I. B.   Not a monistic one—dualistic, perhaps. Machiavelli is to me one of the unintending fathers of anti-monism, because he is the first thinker in my opinion who made it clear that there are two kinds of morality in modern society: there is a pagan morality of *virtù*, of energy, vigorous self-assertion, pursuit of power and glory, Stoic resistance to pain and misfortune, republican boldness, civic patriotism, as in the Roman Republic and the early Empire. The other morality is that of the Christian virtues—humility, unworldliness, preparation for the other world, and submission to secular power in this one, belief in the holiness of sacrifice, of being on the side of the victim not of the victors. Machiavelli does not, of course, specifically say that one morality is preferable to the other; but it is plain which he prefers. He is simply not interested in a purely Christian life. He seems to me the first to make it clear that the very idea of a Christian commonwealth is a contradiction in terms: one cannot be a Christian and an heroic Roman citizen at the same time. Christians must remain humble, to be trampled on at times; Romans resist this successfully. This implies an irreconcilable dualism. One can choose one life or the other, but not both; and there is no over-arching criterion to determine the right choice; one chooses as one chooses, neither life can objectively be called superior to the other. It is a matter of what one wants to do and be. This does open the door to more than two possibilities, indeed, to a pluralist outlook. Montesquieu thought that societies developed under the influence of what he called climate—physical conditions in different lands—and differed accordingly. But in some respects he is not a relativist. He thought of justice as an objective, immutable value. So, too, if you look at Montesquieu's *Journal* when he is travelling, and looks at paintings in Italy, he knows quite clearly what is good and bad—this is not a matter of taste: he allows no relativism in aesthetic judgements. He does say that what is natural and normal in Persia is different from what is customary in France, but in spite of this I think he has a clear idea of virtue, justice, liberty, as absolute values. For him, customs differ, manners vary, but whether this entails pluralism in respect of values is not clear. That remains ambiguous, as, indeed, with Montaigne or Rabelais.

R. J.   How about Russian thinkers like Turgenev and Herzen? Do you consider them founders of pluralism?

I. B.   Turgenev is not a philosophical thinker, he has very few general theories. He is a great novelist, but Herzen was a genuine thinker. He is one of the earliest of those who, perhaps influenced by Romantic theories, thought that we did not discover values but created them, and that the purpose of life was life itself. That is something very different from a great deal that has been thought by the best-

45

known thinkers of the past. For Herzen, life has no purpose beyond itself. Men and women have purposes: but the process of living has none. To ask, as many have done and do, "What is the purpose of life?" is for him not a meaningful question. Purpose implies human beings who conceive purposes; the idea of impersonal purposes—the purpose of life, of nature, of *rerum natura*, no. I know of no one who said this before him in these clear terms, not even Stirner[7], by whom he was probably influenced.

THE PURSUIT OF THE IDEAL

R. J.   What do you think the tasks of political philosophy are?

I. B.   To examine the ends of life. Political philosophy is in essence moral philosophy applied to social situations, which of course include political organization, the relations of the individual to the community, the state, and the relations of communities and states to each other. People say that political philosophy is about power. I do not agree: that is a purely empirical question, settled by observation, historical analysis, sociological enquiry. Political philosophy is an examination of the ends of life, human purposes, social and collective. The business of political philosophy is to examine the validity of various claims made for various social goals, and the justification of the methods of specifying and attaining these. Like all philosophical enquiry it seeks to clarify the words and the concepts in which these views are framed, so that people come to understand what it is that they believe and what their actions express. It sets itself to evaluate the arguments for and against various ends pursued by human

7. Max Stirner (1806–1856), author of *Der Einzige und Sein Eigentum*, originally translated as *The Ego and His Own*.

beings and to prevent what Macmillan, in my recollection, quoted as "talking rot". This is the business of political philosophy and has always been such. No true political philosopher has omitted to do this.

R. J.   In February 1988, after having received the first Prize awarded by the Giovanni Agnelli Foundation, you titled your speech of acceptance at the Turin Opera House "The Pursuit of the Ideal". Can you say a few words on the nature of the "ideal" which you have been pursuing for more than half a century?

I. B.   My talk to the audience at the award of the Agnelli Prize was intended to argue that the pursuit of a single, final, universal solution to human problems was a mirage. There are many ideals worth pursuing, some of them are incompatible with one another, but the idea of an all-embracing solution to all human problems which, if there is too much resistance to it, might need force to secure it, only tends to lead to bloodshed and the increase of human misery. If you ask me what is my own ideal, I can only give you a modest answer. I believe that there is nothing more destructive of human lives than fanatical conviction about the perfect life, allied to political or military power. Our century affords terrible evidence of this truth. I believe in working for a minimally decent society. If we can go beyond this to a wider life, so much the better. But even a minimum of decency is more than we have in some countries.

R. J.   Do you consider yourself a critical humanist?

I. B.   I am not clear about what you mean by these words. I can only say that nobody who believes in either democracy or human rights or a liberal state, as I do, can deny the indispensable need for criticism. Any regime which forbids or limits criticism, save in the most desperate situations in which unanimity is needed to avert total chaos or destruction, is on the way to totalitarianism or some other fanaticism. That is surely obvious, a truism scarcely worth stating.

A BRIDGE TO THE CONTINENT

R. J.   Why do you think French philosophy has been drawn to German rather than to English philosophy?

I. B.   English philosophy has always been drawn to clarity of thought, the tests of theories and hypotheses and analysis of meanings in experience. So, indeed, was French philosophy in the time of Descartes, and indeed until the rise of Bergson. In the 1930s, partly because of the arrival of refugee German philosophers in Paris, it became drawn towards existential problems and Hegelian and post-Hegelian styles of thinking, which Russell and Moore effectively drove out from England early in this century.

R. J.   How do you think there could be a real contact between French philosophy and British philosophy?

I. B.   Most British (and indeed American and Scandinavian) philosophers seem thin and technical to the French, most French philosophers seem opaque and inflated to the English. I wonder if contact could be achieved if, let us say, four first-rate English philosophers and four first-class French philosophers were sent to a desert island for at least three years and compelled to talk to each other about philosophical issues (I have no doubt they could begin by doing so, but they must be persuaded to persist against all obstacles). Then, if any one of these did not understand the others and complained of this and made no concessions, they could be asked simply as a feat of virtuosity to try and talk in the language of each other. If this were promoted, something might be gained. Communication can only be brought about by systematic criticism intelligible to people who talk different languages. The most difficult task for philosophers from different camps is the task of translation. Perhaps it is a hopeless business. But I refuse to be pessimistic. I did make sense of what Alexandre Kojève said about his Marxified Hegel, and of Marcuse too. Although we made friends and talked about music and literature and many other subjects, I could not understand a word of the philosophical writings of, for instance, Theodor Wiesengrund Adorno, who is much admired in France, I am told; nor, I must admit, of my friend Alan Montefiore's friend, Derrida. This may be due to my philosophical conditioning which I am too old to free myself from—I fear that so far as I am concerned it is a hopeless business.

R. J.   May we hope that the translation of your works will be a step forward in this communication.

I. B.   I should be delighted, but I am sceptical. Anglo-American philosophy and Kant formed me. I suspect that my works would seem crudely empirical and primitive to the more sophisticated French thinkers. The chasm remains. My friend Charles Taylor was unable to explain to me what advanced French philosophers wished one to believe or disbelieve; he may be able to bridge it—I cannot. I fear I am too old a dog to learn new tricks.

SECOND CONVERSATION

❖

The Birth
of Modern Politics

MACHIAVELLI: POLITICAL AUTONOMY

RAMIN JAHANBEGLOO   Who chose the title *Against the Current* (was it you or the publisher)?

ISAIAH BERLIN   I did. Because most of the thinkers I wrote about in that book went against the fashionable views of their time. That's why I chose the title *Against the Current*.

They were, for the most part, reactionaries in a period of progressive thought. Of course, some of the thinkers on whom I wrote in this book do not belong to this category. For example, Verdi is very much a man of his time. So was Machiavelli. Machiavelli is a typical Italian Renaissance thinker but he does deviate from one of the central accepted traditional views of the West. I think that Machiavelli was perhaps the first to recognize the possibility of two opposed value systems, the Christian and what is best called pagan. He does not offer an over-arching criterion to determine choice between them. He does not say that either is superior to the other. It is clear that he prefers the values of pagan Rome, but he doesn't condemn or criticize Christianity. We are told that on his death bed, he made a confession, and officially died as a Christian, but the idea which underlies both the *Prince* and the *Discourses*—that there are two kinds of lives which are not compatible, only one of which can create and sustain the kind of State he favours—is an historic moment because it creates a serious rift in the idea of *philosophia perennis* in ethics and politics. The idea that there can be only one true answer to any question, whether of fact or of value, however it is reached, and that the method of discovering the truth is that of rational enquiry, extends from Greece to Rome, from the medieval Schoolmen to the Renaissance, and so to Descartes, Leibniz, Spinoza—to the French *Encyclopédie*, to nineteenth-century thought, and to metaphysicians, Positivists, Realists, Idealists, to all believers in scientific thought in the modern world. Machiavelli was the first thinker who in the same sense allowed that there were at least two ways of life, either of which men could lead, seeking salvation either in this world or the next, which are not compatible. The very idea of a perfect Christian Commonwealth on earth is therefore contradictory; he did not spell this out (that might have got him into serious trouble), but it follows from what he says.

R. J.   Is that the reason why you consider him a pluralist thinker?

I. B.   I regard Machiavelli as a dualist thinker. But once you have two equally valid possibilities you might have more. If there can be two answers, equally "valid", to the same questions, there could be more.

R. J.   But at the end of your essay on Machiavelli, you speak of him as a pluralist thinker?

I. B.   He was a dualist rather than a pluralist thinker, but the point is that he broke a monist tradition. While Machiavelli is the first modern ethical dualist, the first real dualists were some of the Greeks in the fourth century B.C. The greatest philosophers were monists. For Aristotle, in his *Politics*, as for Pericles, as reported by Thucydides, man is naturally involved in the life of the Polis. Pericles allows that some people are not interested in the life of the Polis, they are called *idiotai*; they have opted out, out of society, they are on their own, not exactly crazy, but lacking something, alienated from the normal life of men. For Athenians of the classical period, and for Spartans or Thebans, to participate in the social life of the Polis is a natural function of man. Plato thinks in the same way when he speaks of a desirable society. In the *Republic* and the *Laws*, Socrates, who is critical of the Athens of his time, is nevertheless a good citizen. His war record is excellent. He is not an individualist, though some of his disciples became such. Aristotle describes various kinds of cities, democratic, oligarchical etc. But whatever it may be, even in "bad" cities, everybody is to some degree naturally involved. But with the Stoics and the Epicureans, and before them with Diogenes and the Cynics, this is not so. Stoics declare that you can take part in politics, but that it should not matter to you; do it if you like, or don't—that is not what is of central importance. Epicurus tells you not to take part in political life. Personal salvation is what matters; keep out of politics. There is a break here. These thinkers do not look on politics as intrinsic to human life. The founder of the Stoic school, Zeno, was the favourite of the Macedonian governor of Athens. A kind of chaplain to him. But what he teaches is that the individual should follow reason, and political life is not relevant to the life of reason. So if you do not want to participate in the political life, there is no need to do so. A rather forgotten English scholar, Edwyn Bevan, gives a good example of this. He says: supposing that your master sends you to fetch a parcel from the post office. It is certainly correct for you to fetch it, but if it doesn't arrive, you don't mind; you remain indifferent. So with things which the Stoics describe as indifferent. You can do them, but they are not obligations, they are not part of the rational life. Above all you must not be involved. Because that springs from emotion, and emotion, which distorts reason, must be suppressed.

R. J.   So, who do you consider to be the first pluralists?

I. B.   Not Epicurus and Zeno. They are the first thinkers who allow that there are two forms of life, private and public, but only the natural life should be led. So it is one monism against another: Aristotle against Zeno. Still, the very idea that politics is like sailing, you can do it or not, is the beginning of free choice of how to live: two peaceful philosophical schools, each claiming the authority of reason, in radical opposition; heresy is the mother of pluralism as well as of relativism, the seed of a wider outlook. Aristotle died in 323 B.C., Zeno flourished in about 310 B.C. onwards. So within 15–20 years something radical occurred. Maybe there were other people who said this before. Cynics, Cyrenaics, Sceptics, but nothing before the end of the fourth century has survived, no consistent systems of doctrine. But Stoics and Epicureans were real opponents of the old single communal life. They were rivals of the Academy and the Lyceum, after the death of Plato and Aristotle.

R. J.   Do you consider Plato to have been the first monist?

I. B.   So far as we can tell, yes. There is not much political writing of a coherent kind before Plato. I expect Sophists were monists, but how much do we really know about their politics other than what their opponents report? Plato is the first coherent systematic monist. So are the authors of the Bible. But Machiavelli seems to me to be the first person to indicate a conflict of real values. For Machiavelli you can choose to be a Roman or a Christian, a Roman Stoic or a Christian and a martyr, or at least a victim of those who wield power. That's why I think he is against the current, but I don't think he knew it, he was not a theoretical thinker. He wrote about the state and politics and about how to run a successful republic or principate. His ideas proved shocking not just because—others have done that—he advocates

wicked means to these ends, but because he seems to under-
mine the very idea of a Christian state.

R. J.   Don't you think that your interpretation of
Machiavelli as a thinker "against the current" in some way
goes against the popular opinion on Machiavelli as a
"thinker of power and state"?

I. B.   No, because few interpreters have spoken about
Machiavelli's general view of how life could be lived, that is
not what either he or his interpreters paid attention to. The
ordinary interpretation of Machiavelli is that he said that if
you want a stable and powerful state, you should act in this
or that way. For example, keep the people poor, don't
hesitate to commit crimes, and so on. But they don't stress
the fact that Machiavelli fundamentally makes this incompatible with the life of Christians. He does not deny that,
of course, the best life is Christian, but if you live such a life,
as it is usually understood—a life of humility, free from
worldly ambition—then you must be prepared to be
ignored, oppressed, humiliated, done in. He does not advise
you to avoid this. His advice is for princes or republican
statesmen. In effect he implies that if you are Christian, then I
am not writing for you. A powerful and successful state
cannot be built on the morality of the Gospels. Others may
have believed this, but did not say anything like it.

R. J.   Do you consider Machiavelli an ethical thinker?

I. B.   Yes, he is an ethical thinker, even if he is not interested
in the morality of private life. But I think that political
theory is simply ethics applied to society, to public issues, to
relations of power, that and nothing else. Some people think
that political theory is simply about the nature of power; I
don't think that. I think that political theory is about the
ends of life, about values, about the goals of social existence,

about what men in society live by and should live by, about good and evil, right and wrong. Neutral analysis of the facts of public life is sociology or political science, not political theory or philosophy.

R. J.   In this sense, you feel yourself very close to a thinker like Kant.

I. B.   Yes. Or even Hegel, dare I say it, not very close, but not remote. I am not a Hegelian. Hegel's idea of the state is based on what he calls *Sittlichkeit*, and that is a system or growing development of relations of men to each other, e.g. in the form of a state. His notion of a rational state is based on ideas of what men are and can be and should be. Of course this is opposed to individualist or liberal ethics, the ethics of personal relationships independent of public activity, or of the *vita contemplativa*. It is not that of Pascal, when he said that: "*Tout le malheur des hommes vient d'une seule chose, qui est de ne pas savoir demeurer en repos, dans une chambre.*" But the difference is an *ethical* difference. Pascal is not, and does not mean to be talking about the state. On the contrary, Hegel's moral philosophy is not distinguishable from his political philosophy. But there are some people who say that moral philosophy is one thing, and political philosophy is another. This is said by Croce and many others about Machiavelli. People say that he was not interested in ethics, and that he is amoral, because he is simply concerned with how to maintain an efficient state, that he takes politics away from ethics. This is, I think, a mistake. I think that Machiavelli doesn't separate politics from ethics, only from Christian ethics. Machiavelli is an ethical thinker, he thinks about the ends of life. He wants to know what men should seek. He wants his Italians to return to Roman ideals and practices. He wants the people to be vigorous and patriotic, he believes in *virtù* which is the opposite of softness, *ozio*. *Virtù* means vigour, vitality, ability to endure suffering stoically, strength of purpose, boldness, ambition, the desire to acquire and to keep power; he asks for vigorous, patriotic citizens governed by strong and cunning rulers, intent on power. That is an ethical ideal, civic, humanist, yes, but neither liberal nor democratic, equally distinct from those of John Stuart Mill or Michelet, or Maistre, or Tolstoy, but based on ethical values. I suspect that a Bismarck, Kemal, de Gaulle are the kind of statesmen he might have admired.

R. J.   Do you think that we can speak of two Machiavellis: one of the *Prince* and the other of the *Discourses*? I mean, on one hand an authoritarian Machiavelli, and on the other a republican Machiavelli?

I. B.   No. Machiavelli is a republican, but if you can't have a republic, then it's best to have a good principate than to have a soft, inefficient, weak, incompetent republic. But, of course Machiavelli wants a republic. He was punished by the Medicis for being a republican[1]. He never said that he regretted having been a republican. His letter to the Medicis seeking to get back in favour springs from his wish to come back to public life: the only life he believed in. He wanted a vigorous state, and the best state for him is a strong republic. It also breeds the right view of citizens. But if you can't have a republic, then a principate will do, because the important thing is not to be crushed by another state, by powerful enemies, by predators. Public life can be a jungle: lions and foxes are more likely to survive than rabbits.

R. J.   But it seems to me that Machiavelli is very close to Cicero when he talks about the republic?

I. B.   To a degree. He is not a democrat. By republic he

---

1. In 1513. He rarely left Florence. It was only in 1519 that he regained Lorenzo de Medici's favour.

understands a vigorous state which is conducted for the benefit of the citizens. Of course he doesn't want the people to be humiliated or crushed. Rulers must be both lions and foxes: strong and not gullible, this advice is practical and pragmatic. So he says about Philip of Macedonia, that he drove peoples like cattle—which is not Christian and not even human, but if you want a powerful Macedonian empire, you're driven to do it. The tough Philip and Alexander are preferable to feeble Greek democracies. I do not believe that Machiavelli says that he is not interested in motives or outlook, only offers technical advice—if you want X do Y. No, I think that Machiavelli was passionately in favour of a certain kind of public life, which alone is worth having. He is not just a technical expert.

R. J.   And what do you think about those interpretations which consider Machiavelli to be the first thinker to talk about the autonomy of politics?

I. B.   I have told you that I do not believe in that. I think that politics for him is the application of the kind of moral principles in which he believes, their application to society. Autonomy means that morality has nothing to do with it. Of course, Machiavelli does not discuss ethics. He only says obliquely that what you are doing may be against morality, but in politics necessary. His ethics are pagan, but it is ethics. Talking of autonomy implies that morality is one thing and politics is another. Machiavelli didn't believe in the separation of the two. The reason for advocating a strong republic is that he believes its strength, pride, glory, success are desirable. His outlook is only not compatible with the Christian morality of submission.

R. J.   So, in what way can we consider Machiavelli as a modern thinker?

I. B.   Well, he is the first thinker who realized that there was more than one system of public values. Also he is the first person to discuss international relations. He wanted the public world he lived in better than any other. And before Lenin he asked "who whom?"

R. J.   For you, what are the main characteristics of modernity?

I. B.   I don't think there are characteristics of modernity. I don't know what that means. I don't know where it begins. Pre-modernity, modernity and post-modernity seem to me arbitrary concepts.

THE STATE AND THOMAS HOBBES

R. J.   Well, let us go forward to another political thinker, Thomas Hobbes, whom you never mention in your essays.

I. B.   I am not very interested in Hobbes even though I think that he is a brilliant thinker and a wonderful writer. I have in fact written a little about Hobbes. I once wrote a review of the book by a Marxist—C. B. Macpherson. In his book *The Theory of Possessive Individualism*, he thought that *Leviathan* is not the state or a ruling group but the capitalist class. This seemed to me inaccurate. I doubt if Hobbes thought about the bourgeoisie. I have lectured on Hobbes and have views about Hobbes, Spinoza, Locke and other seventeenth-century political thinkers, but I had no wish to write a book on the history of political theory, consequently I did not write much about them. I was interested in Machiavelli because I am interested in when and how monism, *philosophia perennis*, was first opposed. I read Croce, and he seemed to me to be somewhat conventional, and on

Machiavelli, mistaken. I never understood why Croce dominated Italian intellectual life to so great a degree. Such domination does not seem to be paralleled anywhere else—I know of no comparable case; I find this astonishing. Every modern Italian writer feels obliged to settle his account with Croce, whatever the topic. Some oppose him but they feel they must say why this is so. Of course he was a many-sided writer, he wrote about metaphysics, history, aesthetics, Marxism, many other things, but he cannot be compared to major thinkers—Spinoza or Leibniz, or Kant, or even Hegel or such twentieth-century philosophers as Husserl or Wittgenstein or Russell or William James.

R. J.   In which context do you place the political theory of Hobbes?

I. B.   This seems to me too general a question. Classification is exceedingly tedious.

R. J.   When did you become interested in Hobbes?

I. B.   As a student, of course. I read Hobbes and Locke as I read Descartes and Kant and William James.

R. J.   Do you think Hobbes is a relevant thinker?

I. B.   Well, in a way, yes. I think that history moves in spirals. There are certain people who become interesting because they write about situations which resemble certain later situations. In the nineteenth century nobody thought about Hobbes much, because Victorian England or nineteenth-century France or the United States, or Italy or even Germany did not seem societies to which Hobbes's ideas were naturally relevant. But the twentieth century is politically closer to the seventeenth century. The great violent power struggles, the rise of totalitarian states, the brutality, the danger to individual life, are even greater in this century than they were in the seventeenth. In the seventeenth century, protection against being killed is one of the things that Hobbes talked about. People were afraid of a violent death. The possibility of violent death was more real in seventeenth-century England, for example, than, say, in the England of J. S. Mill. So in our day Hobbes became interesting again. Certain past periods become interesting at certain times. Nobody is interested in third-century Athens, because its problems are too remote from us. On this issue Croce is right: all real questions are in some sense contemporary questions. Hobbes describes an authoritarian state, with stress on laws with no legal method of reform. The reason for obedience to the State is the protection it offers of your security. Fear of death or damage or insecurity are paramount. So in Fascist or other totalitarian states the reason you obey is fear. People followed Mussolini because they feared anarchy, occupation of factories by workers, even liberals like Croce or Toscanini began by favouring Mussolini—though they soon repented. Fear of disorder is Hobbes's major motive. That's why he was against the varieties of opinion, particularly of religion. Sects are like worms in the entrails of the body politic. You must suppress them.

R. J.   So, Hobbes is a monist thinker?

I. B.   Absolutely, more than anybody. Let me tell you something amusing in case it interests you. I used to think that the Soviet Union was a kind of Hobbesian state, because it had harsh laws. But Hobbes doesn't say that all laws have to be harsh. That is a mistake. Hobbes does not want cruelty and oppression, although he has been interpreted in that way. Hobbes wanted rigorous laws, but only the minimum necessary for preserving public order. It's exactly like a man who thinks he may become uncontrolled, and so voluntarily puts on a strait jacket. One wears it, because one thinks one may go mad, and believes that it will protect one. It's like an alarm clock, which you put on in case you fail to wake yourself. If you think you might lose control you invent a machine, Leviathan, whose will automatically restrains you. It is a self-imposed mechanism. That's Hobbes's doctrine. Apropos of this: I went to Paris in 1946 or 1947, and I met there the very interesting thinker, Alexandre Kojève. He was one of the most amusing and intelligent men I have ever met. He had become an important French financial official[2]. We talked about Stalin. I remember I said to him: "What a pity that we know so little about the Greek sophists. Most of what we know about them comes from opponents—Plato and Aristotle, it is as if we only knew Bertrand Russell's views from Soviet text books." "Oh no! If we only knew Bertrand Russell's views from Soviet text books we might think him a serious philosopher!" We talked about Hobbes and the Soviet state. "No," he said, "it is not a Hobbesian state." He went on to say that once one realizes that Russia is a country of ignorant peasants and poor workers, one sees that it is a very difficult country to control. He said that it really was dreadfully backward; backward in 1917, not just in the eighteenth century. Now anyone who wanted to do something with Russia, had to shake it violently. In a society in which you have very severe rules—however absurd—for example, a law which states that everybody has to stand on their heads at half past three, everybody would do this, to save their lives. But that was not enough for Stalin. That would not change things enough, Stalin had to squash his subjects into a dough, which he could knead in any way he

2. Born in Moscow in 1902, Alexandre Kojève died in Paris in 1968. Arriving in France in 1928 with a German doctorate in philosophy, he taught at L'Ecole Pratique des Hautes Etudes from 1933 to 1938. A member of the Resistance (the "combat" group) during the War, in 1946 he was appointed director of foreign relations at the Ministry of Economy and Finance. His lectures on Hegel had a considerable influence on French thought, and notably on Georges Bataille, Jacques Lacan and other well known thinkers.

wanted; there must be no habits, no rules which people could rely on: otherwise things would remain unmalleable. But if you accuse people of breaking laws that they did not break, of crimes that they did not commit, of acts which they could not even understand—that would reduce them to pulp. Then nobody would know where they were, nobody was ever safe, since whatever you did, or did not do you still might be destroyed. That creates real "anomie". Once you have that kind of jelly you can shape it as you choose from moment to moment. The goal was not to let anything set. Kojève was an ingenious thinker and imagined that Stalin was one too. Hobbes conceived the law which if you obeyed, you could survive. Stalin made laws which you would be punished for obeying or not obeying, at random. There was nothing you could do to save yourself. You were punished for breaking or for obeying laws that didn't exist. Nothing could save you. Only out of this passive stuff to which human beings were to be reduced, could the future be built. He said that he wrote to Stalin, but received no reply. I think that perhaps he identified himself with Hegel, and Stalin with Napoleon. He was liable to fancies.

R. J.   I wonder if Hobbes was translated into Russian?

I. B.   Yes. Hobbes in Russian is Gobbs. He is quite well treated in Soviet histories of philosophy, because he was a materialist. Spinoza was also praised, because he too was considered a materialist, absurd as this is. The bad thinkers were Leibniz, Locke, Berkeley, Hume—idealists one and all. Hegel is not condemned entirely because of Marx. Nor was Feuerbach, because, after all, Lenin read him.

SPINOZA AND MONISM

R. J.   Let us move to Spinoza. What do you think of him?

I. B.   I think Spinoza was a complete monist. Unity is good, multiplicity cannot lead you to the truth. His political theory is in some ways like that of Hobbes. From his point of view, in politics you have to govern. In order to govern, a rational person might have to do things which are not strictly honourable. Spinoza is a surprisingly tough-minded political thinker.

R. J.   But he seems to give more power to the people than Hobbes?

I. B.   Yes. But he believes in authority. And, of course, he believed in freedom of thought and expression whereas Hobbes does not. There is a book on Spinoza written by an American ex-Marxist, called *Spinoza and Liberalism*, on these lines. But Spinoza is not a theorist in whom I am particularly interested, because he is too rationalistic for me. But *The Ethics* is a wonderful book, and full of deep insights and noble feeling. It is totally unhistorical: the idea of timeless truths about human beings seems suspect to me.

R. J.   It is the same thing with Descartes or Leibniz?

I. B.   No. Leibniz really is a marvellous universal genius. Moreover he speaks of causes which incline but do not necessitate, which, in the spirit of, I think, Epicurus he calls *Clinamina*. Once you allow deviation from rigid causality, and a multiplicity of individual monads, you are no longer a monist.

R. J.   But what about the theory of the "Best of all Possible Worlds"?

I. B.   That is when he wants to explain why the world is as it is. He says if it had been more perfect, he shouldn't be able to understand it; if it had been simpler, it would have been much cruder. A compromise is made by God, between the most perfect world and the simplest world; this is a kind of *jeu d'esprit*. Leibniz simply believes that God had sufficient reason for all that he creates: nothing is irrational or superfluous. But Dr. Pangloss in *Candide* is a wonderful caricature. No one mocked as brilliantly as Voltaire.

R. J.   So, you don't consider Leibniz as severe a rationalist as Spinoza?

I. B.   Yes, he was, but he conceded more freedom of action and freedom of choice. Spinoza is a rigid determinist, Leibniz is not.

R. J.   But don't you think that Leibniz is a very optimistic thinker?

I. B.   That is true. But Leibniz thinks more in terms of organic development than in mechanical or geometrical terms. For Leibniz entities are *"chargés du passé et gros de l'avenir"*. Leibniz's doctrine is an evolutionary doctrine. It is not the same thing with Spinoza. Spinoza has no sense of change and evolution. He has no sense of history. Spinoza thinks that correct solutions to all questions could have been thought of at any time, but unfortunately weren't, while Leibniz has a sense of the continuity of history, and uniqueness of each moment; Spinoza preaches a kind of timeless rationalism, in a void. He thinks that any idea could have been born at any time. Who in the world has believed this after Hegel?

R. J.   Hegel was very much influenced by Spinoza. Don't you think so?

I. B.   I think Hegel was much more influenced by Aristotle than by Spinoza. As for the influence of Spinoza on Hegel it exists. But the Spinoza of the eighteenth century is not Spinoza; the Spinoza of Herder, the Spinoza of Goethe, is not Spinoza, nor is the Spinoza of Diderot. In the case of the Germans his world turns into an active pantheism; "*Deus sive Natura*" turns into a quasi-mystical doctrine, a romantic approach remote from the dry light of Spinoza.

THE COUNTER-ENLIGHTENMENT: JOSEPH DE MAISTRE AND EDMUND BURKE

R. J.   Let us come back to *Against the Current* and particularly to your essay on the Counter-Enlightenment. What do you think has been the contribution of the Counter-Enlightenment to the development of European thought?

I. B.   Its most important influence on European thought is the belief that science and reason do not have all the answers, that to some central questions of value—ethical, aesthetic, social, political—there can be more than one valid answer. The old belief is that to every question, there can be only one true answer. We may not know it; and we may be too stupid, or too weak or ill-equipped, or crippled by original sin, or unable to find it for some other reason. But if a question is genuine, then there must be one true answer to it. You and I do not know it; but maybe somebody will discover it one day. Perhaps Adam knew it in Paradise; maybe the angels knew it; or if not they, then God alone knows it, but the answers must in principle exist. There must be some right method of getting to the answer. Again, we may not know what the right method is; some look in sacred writings, or Revelation; some look to the Church, others to mathematics or to laboratories or *vox populi*, or the pure heart of a simple peasant or a child (like Rousseau). Salvation depends on finding the right path: hence terrible wars have been fought to save souls, and prevent them from being destroyed by false beliefs. But there must surely be some method of obtaining the true answer. It follows that when all the true answers are obtained, then you can put them side by side, because one true proposition cannot be incompatible with another true proposition—that's logical truth—and then a harmony will result. That is the solution of the jigsaw puzzle. In the case of questions about values that will result in the idea of a perfect life, once you know what that is, you know what to do. That is the monist vision. The Counter-Enlightenment broke through that. The Counter-Enlightenment begins in the eighteenth century in Germany, where people like Hamann said: "God is not a mathematician, God is an artist." In Hamann's case problems could not be answered without grasping the message of the Bible. He thinks that once you begin to question the ethical doctrines of French rationalists, or *philosophes*, you realize that their formulae are too abstract and general to solve the agonizing problems of life. Herder also speaks for the Counter-Enlightenment when he says that "each culture has its own centre of gravity". Herder means by this that different civilizations pursue different goals and they are entitled to pursue them. The fact that we are not Greeks is not against us, the fact that we are not Romans is not a reproach. The idea of trying to make us like the Romans is to distort our proper nature. We are what we are. Our ideals are what they are. Aristotle is theirs, but Leibniz is ours. We cannot return to a remote past. We seek the good, we seek the right, we seek the beautiful and the fact that it does not correspond to what Turks in the Middle Ages, living in a world very unlike ours and faced with problems raised by it, of which we may have little idea, is not relevant to our lives and goals.

R. J.   Who invented the word "Counter-Enlightenment"?

I. B.   An American wrote a book on "Counter-Renaissance". I don't know who invented the concept of

"Counter-Enlightenment". Someone must have said it. Could it be myself? I should be somewhat surprised. Perhaps I did. I really have no idea.

R. J.   In your essay on the Counter-Enlightenment you seem to be more concerned by the thoughts of thinkers like Vico and Herder, than Burke, Maistre or Bonald. Is this because you consider that Vico and Herder are free from reactionary prejudices and hatred of equality and fraternity?

I. B.   I have a long essay on Maistre which will soon be published [*The Crooked Timber of Humanity*, 1990]. He was a frightening but brilliant and important critic of the Enlightenment. Why am I interested in Vico and Herder? Fundamentally, I am a liberal rationalist. The values of the Enlightenment, what people like Voltaire, Helvétius, Holbach, Condorcet, preached are deeply sympathetic to me. Maybe they were too narrow, and often wrong about the facts of human experience, but these people were great liberators. They liberated people from horrors, obscurantism, fanaticism, monstrous views. They were against cruelty, they were against oppression, they fought the good fight against superstition and ignorance and against a great many things which ruined people's lives. So I am on their side. But they are dogmatic and too simplistic. I am interested in the views of the opposition because I think that understanding it can sharpen one's own vision, clever and gifted enemies often pinpoint fallacies or shallow analyses in the thought of the Enlightenment. I am more interested in critical attacks which lead to knowledge than simply in repeating and defending the commonplaces of and about the Enlightenment. You know, it can be tedious to assert again and again that John Stuart Mill was right against Hobbes, or that Sakharov is a nobler thinker than Lenin, or that much that Herzen said is often more true than what was said by Karl Marx. If you believe in liberal principles and rational analysis, as I do, then you must take account of what the objections are, and where the cracks in your structures are, where your side went wrong: hostile criticism, even bigoted opposition, can reveal truth. Hatred can sharpen vision as much as love. I do not share, or even greatly admire, the views of these enemies of enlightenment, but I have learnt a good deal from them; some of the central concepts, and the age of reason, and, above all, of their political implications, are exposed as inadequate, and, at times, disastrous.

R. J.   How about Burke?

I. B.   Well, Burke is an important critic. Like Herder he identified the power and value of tradition in moulding men. Burke's arguments against the French Revolution are very penetrating and prophetic, and have only now been largely accepted, sometimes without admitting it, by most progressive social critics. He must not be blamed for the excesses of some of his modern admirers. One should never blame people for what their views may one day be thought to lead to. To blame Hegel for Nazism is ridiculous, yet people do so. Maistre, yes; he is closer to the *Action française* than Hegel was to Nazism. The great eighteenth-century liberals believed that the way to make people live properly is by education and laws, that is to say, by the method of carrots and sticks. The carrot tempts and the stick coerces. Helvétius thought you could reform society by conditioning people to act rightly by means of rewards and punishments, like training dogs and performing seals. The idea is that once they acquire the habit of living as the educator believes to be the right way, all will be well—happiness, harmony, virtue will flourish. But this goes against Kant's idea of human personality and human freedom, in which I believe. Moulding human beings like children or animals leads logically to Auguste Comte, Marx and Lenin. Once you know what has to be done, you can do it by persuasion or by force and that denies basic human rights—above all of choice—lack of freedom of choice means dehumanization.

R. J.   So do you think that a thinker like Marx is close to a thinker like Maistre?

I. B.   Of course not. On the contrary, Marx is much closer to a thinker like Helvétius, even if he thinks that Helvétius is wrong because he does not deal with economics. These people in the eighteenth century were, like Marx, determinists. But for Marx, they failed to take into consideration central factors, namely the results of the advances of technology, which of course Saint-Simon did. They didn't grasp that all history is the war of classes. Only if you understand that, Marx believed, can you organize things properly. For Marxists, the *philosophes* made quite a few empirical mistakes, but in principle they were right: true forerunners. Plekhanov, who is the most intelligent of all Russian Marxists and an excellent writer, begins his history of Socialism with the *Encyclopédie*, then he moves on to Saint-Simon and Fourier, Rodbertus and Lassalle, and so to Marx and Engels and his own views. Maistre is too black a thinker for Plekhanov, so he ignores him and the other Catholic critics. But Maistre did expose the flaws of naive rationalism and materialism. It is absurd to accept either Maistre or Helvétius, to swallow them whole. One must read both. One must read both Tom Paine and Burke. This is the way to learn something. Nothing is more fatal in ethics or politics than a few simple ideas, as universal keys, however noble, fanatically held.

R. J.   So, from your point of view, there is a great difference between thinkers like Vico and Herder on one side, and Maistre and Burke on the other, even if they are both thinkers of the Counter-Enlightenment?

I. B.   Well, they are similar in the sense that they are all critics of what might be called "optimistic monism". For Vico, there are different civilizations and different scales of value. Herder thought there were different environments, different origins, different languages, different tastes and different aspirations. If you allowed that there can be more than one valid answer to a problem, that in itself is a great discovery. It leads to liberalism and toleration. It leads to the exact opposite of Maistre, and a return to Machiavelli. Nobody was more anti-liberal than Machiavelli, but, paradoxically, his doctrines opened the door to toleration. People sometimes say or act in ways which end in the opposite of what they intended. Maistre was an authoritarian. So was Robespierre. Both went too far and the ideas of both led, or in Maistre's case could lead, to terrible despotism. When you read both, you realize that each uttered truths which conflict. When truths or ultimate values are incompatible with each other, and that no synthesis is possible (it never is, *pace* Hegel), then if the total suppression of one of these truths or basic human goals, and thereby, in some situations, terrible despotism, is to be avoided, a tolerable compromise must be painfully achieved. This is a dull thing to say. If intolerable alternatives are to be avoided, life must achieve various types of often uneasy equilibrium. I believe this deeply: but it is not a doctrine which inspires the young. They seek absolutes; and that usually, sooner or later, ends in blood.

R. J.   And what do you think about Burke's criticism of the French Revolution, as an Englishman? It seems to be very relevant today?

I. B.   Well, of course it is. Burke believed that all things are shaped by tradition. Burke was a Christian. Burke believed that you had to obey the law of God who created Nature to work in certain fashions, and that one has to adjust oneself to the central streams in which the things were moving, and the idea of upsetting deeply rooted traditions in the name of abstract ideas and ideals was futile, dangerous, and morally wrong. This can, of course, if pushed too far, lead to the complete denial of the possibility of radical reform. On the other hand Burke said some very wise things. He said that the idea that there can be discovered such an entity as pure human nature if one strips away all the layers of civilization and art, that you can penetrate to "the natural man", i.e. a creature who embodies what is common and true of all men everywhere, at all times, and nothing beside this, that this idea is false. To make a revolution in the name of true human nature—Rousseau's child of Nature, undistorted by human vice, error, art, science, the corruption of civilization—is absurd and wicked. There is for Burke no such thing as a universal human nature. The arts are part of our nature, civilization is part of our nature, differences of tradition are parts of ourselves. It is not the case that there is a central kernel overlaid by artificial garments—human inventions —art, culture, differences of habit, outlook, taste and character. Nature is growth, not a static unchanging something, the same in all times and places, waiting to be liberated from the accumulation of unnatural integument with which men's vices and foibles have covered it.

R. J.   That's the reason why he is a severe critic of the French Declaration of Human Rights?

I. B.   Of course. The Declaration of Rights of Man and Citizens is one of the noblest legacies of the great Revolution. Nevertheless the idea that, for example, the natural, unlimited right of property is sacred, which Burke, and the French Revolutionaries, I think, believed, is not something that I think I recognize. In today's world we regard private property as indispensable for a minimum degree of individual freedom—Marxist regimes have taught us that—but perhaps neither I, nor most people alive today, would be prepared to die for the capitalist system. In that sense we have advanced beyond the principles both of the Gironde and of the Club des Jacobins.

R. J. Maistre is very close to Burke from that point of view when he says that he has never met anywhere the basic man.

I. B. Oh yes, he has great respect for Burke. Maistre says: I have met Frenchmen, Englishmen, Russians and M. de Montesquieu tells us that there are Persians—but man? Who is he? Of course he is right. Vico said the same thing. Vico denied that there was a general, unvarying human nature. That's why he didn't think that savages had natural law inscribed in their hearts in letters more lasting than brass. When Thomas Paine says about Burke: "He admires the plumage, but forgets the dying bird," there is truth in that too. The *ancien régime* was not to me a particularly attractive regime. The regime of Louis XV does not seem to me better than, say, the regime of Louis-Philippe, or the Third Republic. It was enjoyed by the well-born and the rich; the misery of the poor was appalling: far more than in later times.

R. J. But, philosophically speaking do you feel yourself closer to Burke or to Thomas Paine?

I. B. Neither. I feel close to Condorcet, although he was at times too simple, too politically naive; he said that all questions could be answered by the use of scientific method. *Calculemus* was his formula. They cannot. Human ends conflict, and no amount of calculation can save us from painful choices and imperfect solutions. But his *Esquisse d'un Tableau Historique des Progrès de l'Esprit Humain* is a deeply moving and remarkable work, and much of what he says is new, true and important. What more can we ask of anyone?

R. J.   But, do you agree with his idea of progress?

I. B.   No, but his tone is right. His attitude toward humanity is right. He believed in the Enlightenment, in education, in toleration, and racial and social equality. He believed in a decent human society. But when, against him, Maistre says we are told to follow Nature, but that this leads to curious consequences, what he says is not absurd. The *philosophes* say that Nature is a harmonious whole—if you really study it, Maistre declares, what do you find? A slaughter-house. Plants which destroy each other, animals which rip each other into pieces, violence everywhere, and the worst animal of all is man. Animals of the same species don't often kill each other, but man kills them and his fellow men too—nothing resists him: he is the cruellest of all animals. So, Nature is just a battlefield. That is too overdone perhaps, but it is truer than saying follow Nature, in Nature everything is peaceful and harmonious and beautiful. That is not true. That's why I take an interest in Maistre. As I told you I take more interest in the critics than I take in the champions of all that I believe in.

VICO OR A NEW SCIENCE

R. J.   So, let us go now to one of these champions. What do you think is Vico's significance and relevance for our time?

I. B.   Well, I'll try to explain. Vico is, I believe, the first man, who understood (and told us) what human culture is. He established, without knowing it, the idea of a culture. No one before him, so far as I know, conceived the idea of trying to reconstruct how men and women saw themselves in the surroundings in which they lived, or what they thought (or felt) about nature in relation to themselves, to one another, as creatures persisting through time. He reflected about the essence of differing types of behaviour—of thought, feelings, outlooks, of action and reaction—physical, emotional, intellectual, spiritual, which constitutes cultures. If you want to understand how people lived, you have to know how they worshipped; you have to know what their handwritings were like. You have to know what kind of images, metaphors, similes, they used, how they ate, drank, bred children, conceived of themselves, engaged in personal, social, economic and political life. That is what I think Vico began and Herder continued. The concept of culture as a pattern, not as a single organism, but as a way of existing, is the main contribution of Vico to the history of ideas—that the Roman way of life is different from that of Renaissance Rome; that Roman religion and Roman law have far more to do with each other and tell us more about Roman life than students of either have supposed previously. And so on.

R. J.   In what way do you consider Vico as the ancestor of those who are opposed to the claims of determinists, Positivists and philosophers with a mechanistic view?

I. B.   Vico is not a consistent determinist. He believes in Providence, which determines our lives, but provides us with free will, though not control of the consequences of our actions, which Providence alone arranges. He believes in cycles of historical change, but I think that this is his least original doctrine. Machiavelli and Polybius already believed in cycles. Even Plato believed in something of this kind. But that is not what is interesting in Vico. What is interesting is the idea of the interconnections and inter-illumination of apparently different forms of human thought, behaviour, feeling and action.

R. J. In which way does your interpretation of Vico differ from the romantic view of Vico exemplified by Michelet?

I. B. I think Michelet got it right. Michelet thought that what Vico taught him was that the story of man is the story of groups of people—communities—not of individuals; Vico is not interested in individuals; Michelet followed him in thinking of history as the story of societies fighting against the forces of Nature, and trying to use them to create forms of life in which they can survive and flourish. The story of man as the fight against Nature, against forces, against obstacles human and non-human, that is Michelet's idea of progress towards self-liberation from all kinds of yokes.

R. J. What do you think about the historicist view of Vico associated with the names of Benedetto Croce and Collingwood?

I. B. I do not agree with the historicists' view of Vico; there is a historicism in Vico, if only because of his belief in cycles. One cannot doubt that. But I don't feel close to the interpretations given by Croce or Collingwood: they used Vico for their own purposes.

R. J. You seem to be very close to Collingwood, when he says that "*Vico was actually too far ahead of his time to have very much immediate influence*"?

I. B. Yes I am. That is so. Vico was a thinker who was in advance for his time. There are authors who deny this, and say that Vico was a typical Neapolitan thinker of his time. I disagree. On this I agree with Collingwood. Vico's ideas only began to be understood in the nineteenth century. Vico was discovered late; he was a prophet before his time. He is really one of the few true cases of the romantic image of the unsuccessful artist or lonely thinker, neglected in his day, until later generations realize what a genius he was.

R. J.   In your essay "The Divorce between the Sciences and the Humanities" you speak of Vico as a thinker who revealed for the first time the great divide between the provinces of natural science and the humanities.

I. B.   Yes. Vico was the man who said that everybody talks about Nature, but what do we know about Nature? We know what we see, hear and touch, but don't know why things happen as they do. The point is that in the case of mankind we can imagine, have an insight into, what makes people want what they want. I don't know what it is to be a table. I don't know what it is to be electric energy. But I do know what it is to feel, think, hope, fear, question, be puzzled, be ashamed. Dogs can't feel remorse. To that extent they are opaque to me. But I can understand what you mean. I can grasp what you want to say without using experimental methods to establish what your gestures or words are meant to, or in fact, convey: we recognize such "understanding" as different from scientific or common sense "knowing"; that's what Dilthey called "Verstehen" as different from "Wissen". Now, Vico is the first person who discovers "understanding" as being different from knowledge e.g. of the external world. We talk about Nature, but what we know about Nature is what we discover about the external world. We see and feel our bodies; but we can also tell what it feels like to be an embodied human being, of this we have an "inside" view; not just as observers, but as actors, and that is what the New Science is about. Understanding is about purposes, feelings, hopes, fears, efforts, conscious and unconscious, while science is about the behaviour of bodies in space. In other words, we know what it is to look like a table. We don't know what it is to be a table. To understand past cultures is to understand what these people were after. How they saw themselves in relation to others. How they saw the world and how they saw themselves in the world. Our methods are not similar to those of physics: the point is that we can know—understand—more about ourselves, than we can know about Nature, which we observe or manipulate but cannot understand, cannot grasp from within, as actors.

R. J.   In your essay "Vico and the Ideal of the Enlightenment" you point out the fact that the conflict between monism and pluralism became a central issue through Vico's thought. Do you consider Vico to be the first thinker of pluralism in the history of Western thought?

I. B.   No, the idea of variety is at least as old as Xenophanes and Herodotus. The seventeenth and eighteenth centuries are monistic centuries. But simply because Vico was interested in progression of cultures and distinguished one culture from another not positivistically but teleologically, because of that he laid the foundations of stress on differences and not on similarities; and that is the root of pluralism.

R. J.   Do you agree with Karl Löwith for whom Vico's doctrine of "verum-factum" is influenced by Aquinas and Thomism?

I. B.   No. The doctrine of "verum-factum" is influenced, not by Thomism but by Augustine. Augustine says that God alone fully knows what d he makes. Knowledge and creation are one. God knows the world since His knowledge made it, we do not know it because we didn't make it. But of course, Vico is a Catholic. Vico moved among priests, and was politically no doubt an anti-Enlightenment reactionary in his own time. Marxists want to deny that, if only because Karl Marx said that Vico did for the evolution of consciousness what his doctrine does for historical change. So, too, Trotsky mentions Vico favourably, I think on the first page of the *History of the Russian Revolution*. Hence Vico has been recognized in the Soviet Union. But fundamentally Vico was of course a sort of dissident Catholic. He was not a Thomist, because Thomism believes in inborn knowledge of natural laws, while Vico did not: he thought men learnt these truths—barbarians did not possess them.

R. J.   For you, Vico has at least one forerunner, who is Nicholas of Cusa?

I. B.   Yes. He did say something similar. I can't quite remember what, I don't think that Vico mentions him.

ON HANNAH ARENDT

R. J.   Do you agree with Hannah Arendt, when she says that: "Vico, who is regarded by many as the father of modern history, would hardly have turned to history under modern conditions. He would have turned to technology, for our technology does indeed what Vico thought human action did in the realm of history"?

I. B.   What wonderful nonsense! Of course it is true that if Vico were alive today, he would have paid attention to technology because it is a central factor in the evolution of our civilization. Anyone today who is interested in civilization is bound to take into account technological change. One of the truest things which Marx ever expounded was the powerful influence of technological factors on the way people live, and think, and act, in other words on their entire culture. Of course Saint-Simon said it before, but Marxists tend to slide over that. Marx took notice of Saint-Simon, as he did of Vico. There is no doubt that Vico would have taken an interest in the influence of the technological change on our culture. But the idea of technology today replacing his interest in history, in the many strands of human activity, of the rich web of historical movement is a typical lack of understanding on the part of the egregious Hannah Arendt. I do not greatly respect the lady's ideas, I admit. Many distinguished persons used to admire her work. I cannot.

R. J.   Why?

I. B.   Because I think she produces no arguments, no evidence of serious philosophical or historical thought. It is all a stream of metaphysical free association. She moves from one sentence to another, without logical connection, without either rational or imaginative links between them.

R. J.   Have you read any of her books?

I. B.   Yes, I have tried to read several of her books since some of my friends praised her to me. The first book I looked at was *The Origins of Totalitarianism*. I think that what she said about Nazis is correct, if not new; but on the Russians she was mostly wrong. Then I read *The Human Condition*, it seems based on two ideas, both historically false. The first is that the Greeks did not respect work, but that Jews did. Now, it is true that for Aristotle manual workers, still less slaves, could not create a true Polis, because they didn't have the education, the leisure and the wide horizons of the *Megalopsychoi*—grandees, the "magnanimous", men of wide vision. They were too driven, their lives and outlooks were too narrow. Plato did not, I suspect, much like the proletarian outlook and form of life either. But apart from them there is no doctrine, so far as I know, about work among the Greeks. There was actually a minor God of work,

Ponos, to be found in Greece. Moreover, she distinguished work—creative, good—from labour, mechanical, repetitive, not truly worthy of respect. But Heracles is a demi-God, and yet he does not refrain from the lowest forms of labour—clearing out stables, strangling hydras. She says somewhere, I seem to remember, that the low-grade workers in Athens had no vote. Socrates made funerary monuments, Cleon, the great demagogue, was a tanner. So much for that. Now the Jews: for Jews work is a curse; the Bible says that because of the Fall of Adam "from the sweat of thy brow" must we make our living. The Talmud says that the fact that you are a manual worker may not stop you from being a great rabbi. So you must honour great teachers who may be cobblers or carpenters—but there is no merit in work as such, it is a necessity. In the ancient world, if you didn't need to work, that was your good fortune. There is nothing against the rich, as such. The Hebrew prophets do not denounce riches, only the wicked things the rich and powerful do. The idea that you have to work, *laborare est orare*, is a Christian doctrine. Fichte, Schiller, celebrate work—as a creative act, the artist imposing his personality on the raw material—what has this got to do with Homer, Sophocles, Isaiah, Rabbi Akiva[3]?

R. J.   Hannah Arendt is in fact very much influenced by the German thinkers.

I. B.   She seems to be influenced by nobody else. She was, one is told, very much influenced by Heidegger and Jaspers. But I have not yet discovered something of hers which I find arresting, which stimulates thought, or illuminates one: Auden, Lowell, Mary McCarthy, who admired her, what did they derive from her? When I asked Auden about this, he

3. Rabbi born in Roman occupied Judaea in AD 50, who adopted an original method of mystical interpretation of the Bible and a systematic classification of the "Mishna". He died in AD 150.

remained silent and changed the subject. Mary McCarthy edited her posthumous lectures but never told us what difference this made to her own ideas. All very odd.

R. J.   Have you read her book called *The Jew as a Pariah*? She is very close to you with regard to Herder, for example.

I. B.   No, I have not read it, but you frighten me when you say that she is close to me.

R. J.   Do you dislike her because she was not a Zionist?

I. B.   No. She was a fervent Zionist when I first met her.

R. J.   When did you meet her?

I. B.   I met her in New York in 1941 with a friend of mine called Kurt Blumenfeld, a leader of German Zionists. She was working at that time for an organization which tried to get Jewish children out of Germany to Palestine. At that time she seemed to me a hundred per cent Zionist. On the second occasion, when I met her, about ten years later, she attacked Israel. She was perfectly entitled to change her mind—I had nothing against that. It is her ideological writings that repelled me. Gershom Scholem, the great Jewish scholar, knew her well. He had a polemical encounter with her.

R. J.   Was it about Arendt's book, *Eichmann in Jerusalem*?

I. B.   Yes. I am not ready to swallow her idea about the banality of the evil. I think it false. The Nazis were not "banal". Eichmann deeply believed in what he did, it was, he admitted, at the centre of his being. I asked Scholem why people admired Miss Arendt. He told me that no serious thinker did so, that people who admired her were only the

"littérateurs", only men of letters, because they were unused
to ideas. For Americans she represented continental thought.
But, he declared, anybody who was truly cultivated and a
serious thinker could not abide her. Scholem thought that,
and he had known her since the early twenties.

ON BEING JEWISH TODAY

R. J.   Do you consider yourself a Zionist?

I. B.   Yes, certainly. I was not converted to Zionism. I was
a Zionist even as a schoolboy. My parents were not Zionists
in Russia. I drifted into it as something quite natural. I
thought it was right. I realized quite early in my life that
Jews were a minority everywhere. It seemed to me that there
was no Jew in the world who was not, in some degree,
socially uneasy. Jews feel uneasy even if they are well treated,
even if they are genuinely "integrated" and have friends
everywhere. There always remains some small sense of social
uneasiness. I do not think that there is a country where Jews
feel totally secure, where they do not ask themselves: "*How
do I look to others?*", "*What do they think of me?*" Persians are
not interested in the way Turks look on them. Chinese are
not worried about how Indians think of them. Goethe was a
great German poet. He wrote about life, love, sorrow,
poetry, science, ideas, thought. Because he was a German, he
was a great German poet. Heine was also a German poet, but
he mainly wrote about what it is to be a German. That is
because Heine was not fully accepted by Germans, and didn't
feel comfortable about his being a Jew. Despite his con-
version to Christianity, he was troubled by this, and that is
typical of what I mean. Heine talks about Germans and
Germany; Felix Mendelssohn, the composer, also behaved
like a convert to Germanism; it was he who revived Bach
and German Lutheran music; Schumann and Brahms did

not feel the need for re-creating a German tradition. There must be somewhere, I felt, where Jews were not forced to be self-conscious,—where they did not feel the need for total integration, for stressing their contribution to the native culture—where they simply could live normal, unobserved lives. The purpose of Zionism is normalization; the creation of conditions in which the Jews could live as a nation, like the others. Alexandre Kojève, whom I spoke of before, once said to me: "*The Jews have the most interesting history of any people. Yet now they want to be what? Albania? How can they?*" I said: "For the Jews to be like Albania constitutes progress. Some 600,000 Jews in Romania were trapped like sheep to be slaughtered by the Nazis and their local allies. A good many escaped. But 600,000 Jews in Palestine did not leave because Rommel was at their door. That is the difference. They considered Palestine to be their own country, and if they had to die, they would die not like trapped animals, but for their country." That's what I mean. I don't want Jews to stop living where they live. If they do not mind being a minority, that is in order. There is nothing wrong with being a minority. Some people feel minorities to be a disturbing element—T. S. Eliot, for example, or the French *intégralistes* who influenced him. Minorities are often a valuable stimulus to the majority, a leaven, a source of fermentation. But nobody should be forced to be a minority. If you don't want to belong to a minority, and you want a normal life, you can fully attain it only in a country whose culture is yours. This path must be opened.

R. J.   Do you think that the foundation of the state of Israel has solved the Jewish problem?

I. B.   For individual Jews, no. Not the personal problem, but the political problem, yes. Israelis do not feel uneasy about themselves. They certainly face other problems and very serious ones, but they feel comfortable in their own skins. That's what I mean. The experiment succeeded against all the odds. Even the American Jews who supported Israel feel themselves less foreign in America than they did in the 30s. Just as Greeks have Greece, Germans have Germany, so Jews have a homeland in Palestine, in Jerusalem. Psychologically it is a substitute homeland. Most Polish Jews cannot feel rooted in Poland. If Jews don't have real geographical roots, they are made happy by imagining ones—by an enormous act of psychological self-transformation, by being decolonized.

R. J.   Don't you want to go and live in Israel?

I. B.   Too late for me, because I don't speak Hebrew freely: I am too old to cut myself off from my present way of life. When I go to Israel I do feel free, I do not feel that I am in a foreign country. In Israel I don't particularly feel a Jew, but in England I do. I am neither proud nor ashamed of being a Jew. I am as I am, good or bad. Some people have dark hair, others have blond hair, some people are Jews as some people are Welsh. For me being a Jew is like having two hands, two feet, to be what one is. Israel is a country where I have a natural affinity with the inhabitants. I remain totally loyal to Britain, to Oxford, to Liberalism, to Israel, to a number of other institutions with which I feel identified.

R. J.   What do you think about the problems of Israel?

I. B.   Politically there are many very grave problems. I think that the present government has made terrible mistakes. I am not a supporter of Mr Shamir, Mr Sharon or Mr Begin. I think they have done great harm to Israel, culturally, morally, politically, materially.

R. J.   Do you think that there has to be a reconciliation with the Palestinians?

I. B.   Of course. This is true, but it does not make it unnecessary, indeed, makes it urgent, to make a positive effort to compromise. Understanding people who oppose us is what Herder taught us.

HERDER AND THE VISION OF SOCIETY

R. J.   You find a striking resemblance between the views of Vico and Herder, even if you do claim in your essay "Herder and the Enlightenment" that Herder had read Vico's *La Scienza Nuova* at least 20 years after his own theory of history had taken shape.

I. B.   There are various hypotheses about the connection. I don't find them totally convincing. There was Cesarotti, who had read Vico and wrote commentaries on Ossian and Homer. So Herder could have got Vico's ideas on Homer, for example and what these imply, from Cesarotti whom he speaks about. That is the hypothesis of Professor Clark of Texas. Then I discovered an Italian, Conte Calepio, who certainly knew Vico's ideas at first hand. He corresponded with the Swiss scholar Bodmer, who wrote about German sagas and folk tales. Bodmer, Breitinger, and others revived interest in the Song of the Nibelungs and primitive poetry generally. They studied primitive song and the literature of what had been regarded as barbarian peoples. That is also a possible bridge between Vico and Herder. Then there was Bishop Lowth in Oxford, a professor of Hebrew. He said that the Old Testament was the epic poetry of the Judaean people. This is a new idea, echoed by Herder. But contact between Vico and Herder has never been properly established. Herder mentions Vico for the first time, as I said, 20 years after he had formulated his own ideas about history, in a fairly complete form by 1773, or even earlier.

Some years before, Goethe gave a copy of the *New Science* to Jacobi. So if there is an influence, it is not direct—at best through intermediary scholars. Anyway, ideas of influence are always quite difficult to trace. But the similarities of outlook are, in this case, pretty startling.

R. J.   You consider that "Herder's vision of society has dominated Western thought, but the extent of its influence has not always been recognized because it has entered too deeply into the texture of ordinary thinking". Is this the main reason why Herder is ignored by contemporary thought?

I. B.   I think so. He is either ignored or attacked. He is usually known as the father of German nationalism. He is considered by some anti-nationalists as having anticipated Fichte, Hegel, Bismarck, Lueger, the Kaiser and ultimately Nazism. Herder is indeed the first person to emphasize that the need to belong to a community is a basic human need, just as strong as that for eating, drinking, warmth, security, but he was deeply anti–imperialist and anti-nationalist. There are certain philosophers who identify certain basic psychological facts, not clearly named before, and only described and formulated later, and so becoming topics of discussion. For example Hegel can be said to have pointed out the human need for recognition; that men want others to recognize their status, needs, character as an individual, independent entity. I do not want you to behave to me as if I were dependent, a slave, I claim the rights you claim for yourself. Recognition is something that people clearly demand. Of course, if you had asked Greeks or Romans, they might, if you used appropriate expressions, have understood what you meant. But nobody ever spoke of this in clearer language than Hegel about *Anerkennung*. As for Herder, everybody has always known that people belong to tribes, and that they are not happy in exile. That is not exactly new. But Herder, so far as I know, was the first person who said that to belong to a community was an essential need. He may have over-emphasized this, as discoverers often do. But he understood this basic need. For him "to belong" means that people understand what you say without your having to embark on explanations, that your gestures, words, all that enters into communication, is grasped, without mediation by the members of your society. I remember that a friend of mine, who came from the Balkans and had lived in England for 40 years, said to me: "Solitude doesn't mean that you live far from other people. It means that people don't understand what you are saying." That's a penetrating observation. Of course people understand others from remote places or times, to some degree: but not in the direct instinctive way in which people who live together normally communicate. That is why Herder thinks that it is language, habits, gestures, instinctive reactions, that create unity and solidarity—distinctive outlooks, cultures, social wholes. The way in which Portuguese eat, drink, walk, speak, get up, and their laws, their religion, their language, all that we call typically Portuguese, possess a certain pattern, a Portugueseness, which does not fit corresponding German behaviour. It may be that the Portuguese conception of law or history, and the German conception of these things may resemble each other, but they belong to basically different patterns of living. Whatever their similarities, Portuguese cannot feel totally at home in Germany: and nostalgia, craving for home, is universal and "the noblest of all pains". The idea of what moves families, milieux, societies, nationalities, is deeply influenced by Herder. That's why Herder for example, influenced the Jews and the southern Slavs directly or indirectly, because he articulated their sense of identity which earlier theorists, perhaps only the forgotten Vico and the remote Montesquieu had stressed.

HISTORY OF IDEAS: A LONELY DISCIPLINE

R. J.   Speaking of solitude, do you consider yourself a lonely philosopher?

I. B.   As a philosopher I was not lonely. When I taught philosophy at Oxford I was a member of a group of philosophers, we all spoke the same language, we discussed the same topics, I was very much part of a movement. Of course I was critical of the Positivist bias of it in some ways, but I belonged to it. Then my interests changed. The history of ideas is not fashionable in British academic life. In fact I became intellectually somewhat isolated. There are not many people I could or can talk to about this. This is not a subject in which the English take much interest. Maybe it does not interest people who assume that their ideas are universally accepted, hence they do not bother to understand their history. The French surely still think that French ideas are of universal significance; French culture is simply culture itself; that people who were not illuminated by *le rayonnement français* were simply unfortunate. Yet there are histories of French ideas, particularly of political and social ideas, books called "From Bodin to Montesquieu", "From Montesquieu to Rousseau", "From Rousseau to Saint-Simon" and on to Léon Bourgeois, Jaurès, Sartre. For example, let us suppose that you were a cultivated Peruvian or Indian in the nineteenth century. To be cultivated meant that you must at least have heard of, even if not read, Adam Smith, and possibly Bentham—it would be as well if you did. Certainly John Stuart Mill, Burke, Carlyle, Darwin, Spencer, Buckle, even Ruskin were regarded as major thinkers. The English made a central contribution to the dominant ideas of the nineteenth century, no matter whether you accepted it or not—of the Germans, the Peruvian should have heard of Hegel, and Marx and Nietzsche, possibly

Schopenhauer—of the French, Rousseau, Michelet, Taine, and perhaps, but not necessarily, Renan. Yet, so far as I know, there is not a single well known book about the history of English thought. Of course, there are one or two books on English philosophy in the technical sense. But on the history of general ideas from Bacon to Hobbes and Locke, to Burke and Hume, from Hume to Mill,—and so to Ruskin, Newman, Arnold, Tawney, Russell—only monographs. On the links between them all, or the absence of links, nothing. There is, I believe, an obscure book on some of this—published I don't know when; nobody refers to it. I don't say that the history of ideas of a given country—from thinker to thinker, is necessarily a good book to write, such books usually slide over individual ideas, without paying enough attention to the essential significance of any of them—Kuno Fischer's history of German philosophers from Kant to Fichte to Schelling to Hegel is not worth reading. Still it is significant that the Germans have what they call *Geistesgeschichte*, *Ideengeschichte*, and so on; so do the French: American universities have Chairs in "American Intellectual History". But in England I doubt if there are more than two or three scholars working in this field. For that reason, I feel isolated. This cannot be helped. I do my best in a corner of history neglected in my country. This is, I am afraid, a very long answer, to a very short question.

❖

Political Ideas:
The Test of Time

ON COMMISSION OR IN THE CAB RANK

RAMIN JAHANBEGLOO   You once compared yourself to a tailor who doesn't work without getting commissions. But I don't think that your essays are a result of pure chance. Do you feel very close to the thinkers whom you work on?

ISAIAH BERLIN   No, it is not pure chance. I do not do all I am asked to do. I refuse more orders than I accept. I reflect, at times, on how I came to work on Vico and Herder. The piece on Vico I wrote because I was asked to say something about him by the Italian Institute in London. I knew the head of the Institute and he asked me to give a lecture on some Italian topic. I love Italy and Italians. I said to myself "Why not?" But the Italians are not rich in first-class thinkers,— who, apart from Machiavelli, Vico and Croce? Marsiglio of Padua? Pomponazzi? Pareto? Compared to Descartes? Leibniz? Kant? Wittgenstein? So I chose Vico, a deeply original thinker, whose genius was fully appreciated only long after his time.

R. J.   Do you consider Dante a thinker?

I. B.   I am not much good on religious philosophy—but *De Monarchia* is an important political treatise. At that level Marsiglio of Padua is an important thinker too. So too is

Beccaria. There were Italian thinkers during the Enlightenment period and during the eighteenth century. But in properly called philosophy, Vico is the most original philosopher the Italians have produced. Michelet and Sorel had acclaimed him as a genius, so I began reading Vico; I was duly fascinated; so I thought I might say something about him. I began to lecture on him at Oxford. I think my lecture on him in London was produced originally in Italian, in Rome, and subsequently printed in English. The same was the case with Herder. I was asked to give a lecture at Johns Hopkins University in Baltimore. They said they wanted something on the philosophy of history. I had been reading Herder, because I was interested at that time in the origins of European nationalism. So that's how it all started. It always starts with a commissioned lecture or paper.

THE HUMILIATION OF THE GERMANS

R. J.   In your essay on Herder, you describe him as "an early and passionate champion of variety" and "one of the earliest opponents of uniformity". Can you clarify this idea?

I. B.   I'll try. The central idea of Herder's doctrine is the wide variety of national and cultural traditions. He is not a nationalist, although he has been accused of, and praised for, nationalism. This is a mistake. When he says *national* and *Nationalgeist* one must understand national culture, not political self-assertion. Even that is a reaction to the patronizing attitude to the Germans by the French. I believe that the Romantic Movement which begins in Germany was influenced by the systematic humiliation of the Germans, the *de haut en bas* view of them in Paris. I have an *idée fixe* about this which might be untrue, like most *idées fixes*. My view is that the Germans did not have a true Renaissance. I don't think you'll find that in books by German historians, but I think that it is true. Let me give you an example of what I mean. If you had travelled across Europe, from let us say, Lyon, to, for example, Vienna in, say, 1500, you would have found that in France there was a high culture even in the southern provinces. There were poets and painters at that time in France. Italy was in the full glory of the High Renaissance. In Germany you would have found Dürer, Grünewald, and other excellent painters and splendid scholars like Reuchlin and his friends. Now supposing you performed this journey around 1600. In France the Parnassiens, the Libertins, the readers of Montaigne and Rabelais. In the Low Countries, painters of the highest genius. In England Shakespeare, Marlowe, Bacon and a great flowering. In Spain Cervantes, El Greco, Velazquez, Lope de Vega, in Italy Mannerists, Galileo, poor Giordano Bruno burnt in that year as a heretic. New stirrings in Sweden and Poland. But what went on at that time in Vienna or Germany? Scarcely anything to be remembered. There was one original genius—Kepler in Denmark and Munich. Who had ever heard of him then? Or of Jakob Boehme, a Silesian cobbler? The first admired German was Heinrich Schütz, a gifted composer. And possibly Althusius (Althaus). The real rise was with Leibniz in the later seventeenth century. In between only *Simplicissi-mus*. Usually the real reason for this decline is given to be the Thirty Years War. But the Italians were also invaded by the French, and still a rich Italian culture continued. Defeats don't necessarily stop cultures. Of course there were poets in Germany, but Germany was very much not a top nation at that time, as were France, above all, and Spain, England and Italy.

R. J.   What role do you think was played by the Reformation in the rise of German culture?

I. B.   I wonder. I am not a historian, but I have the impression that it did something to abort the Renaissance in

Germany. There is a great upward movement among the Germans in, say, 1470–1510 but by 1580? 1600? Althusius? Kepler? Boehme? Not a cultural movement. If I ask you what caused the Renaissance in Florence you will give me reasons. You will tell me, it was a flourishing city, with a lot of trade, religion declining, the rise of secular studies etc. But even if you knew all that by 1350, you would still not be able to predict the great heights of the Italian Renaissance in the fifteenth and sixteenth centuries. Historical explanations elucidate something—outline possibilities, potentialities, but cannot predict on the basis of some historical pattern; they don't take the form of first A, then B, then C, as in Karl Marx or in Hegel. I don't know what the cause of German cultural decline is. Maybe it's the Reformation. But in the Netherlands there was a Reformation too, and yet great painters, artistic geniuses, great jurists, Erasmus and his followers. It is rather mysterious, even Poland was more productive, e.g. in Latin poetry in that period. And again Spain, France, England—unbelievable flowering. I think that the humiliation of the provincial Germans by the pride and power of Paris is an important factor. The result of cultural hegemony by others is usually the same. First you feel inferior, then you start imitating the top nation, then you revolt against the imitation, and you ask why must we imitate or ape others; we surely have our own culture. That is what is happening in Africa nowadays. The first true, strong German reaction against French culture is pietism. It is a profound spiritual movement. The pietists in effect say: "Let the French have their painting, their music, their architecture, their polite Abbés conversing with noble ladies in the Salons. All that is dross, of no value, even contemptible. The only thing that truly matters is the soul, man's relation to God and to himself, nothing else matters. The inner spirit, the depths of the individual soul, *Innerlichkeit*—that alone is real: ceremony, learning, hierarchy, are not what matters. So pietists reject ecclesiastical discipline; a profound religious movement follows, and Bach and Kant, Herder and Lessing and Hamann are shaped by it. Most German school teachers and professors of that time were influenced by pietism and by the search for *Innerlichkeit*, the inner life—in its religious and, later, secular forms. Herder was only the most typical product of this vision, especially when he declares that each civilization has its own, unique, individual spirit—its *Volksgeist* from which everything flows, which creates and understands what it creates.

HERDER, NATIONALISM AND ZIONISM

R. J.   Well, people speak of Herder as a nationalist thinker, but in your own opinion Herder's nationalism is not political. You consider Herder's conception of a good society is closer to the anarchism of Thoreau or Proudhon, than to the ideals of Fichte, Hegel or the political Socialists?

I. B.   No, he is a democratic, anti-imperialist populist, a forerunner of the Russian and Central-European populist radicals. Herder rejects passionately the value of conquest. He rejects the idea of the superiority of one nation to another. The proposition that "my nation is superior to yours", which is the root of aggressive nationalism, is false for Herder. Every nation has a full right to its own individual development. Herder optimistically believed that all the flowers in the human garden could grow harmoniously, that cultures could stimulate one another and contribute to a creative harmony. That is not how it turned out historically. But Herder is incurably optimistic and idealistic. There is no political nationalism in Herder, because political nationalism inevitably leads to aggression, it feeds national pride, and he hates that. Among his villains were Alexander the Great and Julius Caesar and Romans generally, because they crushed other people's civilizations, for example, in Asia Minor.

Only the Jews survived, but only if transplanted to their native soil, i.e. Palestine, could they rise again as a nation. He believes in peace, unlike Proudhon, who liked war. But still, you are right, because Herder is close to people who believe in devolution; he is against all forms of centralization; that is why he hated the Holy Roman Empire, because it forced disparate, dissimilar nations into an artificial combination. He is against Frederick the Great, because he sent French officials to lift the economic life of East Germany, and these French were often contemptuous of what they considered a primitive Prussian population, which provoked an anti-French reaction in East Germany particularly; Herder is a victim of this particular Francophobia.

R. J.   Speaking of nationalism, I think that for you nationalism is an ideology in which there exists a similarity between the life of a society and that of a biological organism?

I. B.   No, I wish to reject that metaphor. Analogies of this type between individuals and groups can lead to dangerous fallacies. In particular biological metaphors have led to irrational and brutal forms of nationalism and intolerance. There is, of course, such a thing as the growth and development of a nation, a society, but that is just a metaphor. Of course nations are not biological organisms, their texture is something very different, linguistic, historical, psychological.

R. J.   You also speak of the infliction of a wound on the collective feeling of a society as a necessary condition for the birth of nationalism.

I. B.   Well, that's a metaphor too. Infliction of a wound means humiliation either by a military conquest or an infliction of injustices or oppression of some kind, where one nation or group is humiliated by another. This usually leads to what I call the nationalist reaction—the painful "bent twig" phenomenon. If it is bent a twig lashes back. But the biological metaphors used by Hegel can lead to terrible consequences.

R. J.   Hegel's *Volksgeist* for example?

I. B.   No, *Volksgeist* is harmless and embodies an important concept. *Volksgeist* was invented by Herder. For Herder a nation is not a state, but a cultural entity of people who speak the same language, they live on the same soil, and possess the same habits, a communal past, common memories. Herder says nothing about blood, or biological continuity, or any genetic factors. Herder was fundamentally against all racist ideas.

R. J.   But what makes you think that nationalism is still alive in European thought today?

I. B.   Oh, but it is one of the most powerful movements in the world today. Among the many things that the prophets in the nineteenth century foresaw, the growth of nationalism is not mentioned. They believed that nationalism was declining, they thought that once the great empires—the Austro-Hungarian Empire, the Russian Empire, even the British and French Empires—were destroyed, the constituent peoples would peacefully develop their own national form of self-government. Mazzini was a kind of Herderian. He didn't talk about races, I don't know if Mazzini ever read Herder, because I don't know if he was translated into Italian, but he was, of course, translated into French by Edgar Quinet. But, as I said, acute nationalism is just a re-action to humiliation, and top nations don't experience that. Nationalism is a reaction to wounds. Let us take for example England. England was not invaded or seriously defeated for eight hundred years. So when English nationalism grew with the Empire, it was not strong. But so far as there is such a thing as English chauvinism, it is the result of the weakening of imperial bonds leading to the loss of Empire. In France, extreme nationalism arose as a result of the defeat of 1870. There is French nationalism in the mid century but it becomes acute only in 1870–80, with Barrès, Maurras and the *Action française*. The Dreyfus case is the belated result of the humiliation of the Franco–Prussian war. There was national pride but not much real nationalism under Louis-Philippe. When a Frenchman said: "*Je suis un bon patriote*" during the French Revolution, this did not mean: "I am a member of the French nation," but "I believe in Liberty, Equality and Fraternity, which is the proud and noble doctrine of my revolutionary country." It means "I am in favour of the wonderful libertarian ideas which my country has proclaimed." It doesn't mean "I am proud of my French blood or race."

R. J.   What do you think about nationalism in a doctrine of a philosopher like Fichte?

I. B.   He certainly became a fervent nationalist, perhaps in reaction to the Napoleonic Conquests, and in Fichte there is much more nationalism than there was in France in his day. He is the father of political romanticism, and romanticism is what nationalism came out of.

R. J.   Don't you think that nationalism represents a danger for democracy in today's world?

I. B.   Of course. It is a danger to everything. Nationalism simply means that we say to ourselves that nobody is as good as we are, that we have a right to do certain things solely because we are Germans or Frenchmen. Once you invoke infallible impersonal authority like the nation, this extends to the Party or the class, or the Church, the path is then open to oppression.

R. J.   Do you think Zionism is also a nationalistic feeling?

I. B.   Yes, of course. Today Zionism has unfortunately developed a nationalistic phase. The origins of Zionism were very civilized and Herderian. The Jews wanted simply a way of life which was Jewish, not necessarily dominated by religion, but as a community bound by many secular ties. The Jews wanted a framework in which they could freely develop as a community, without fear of persecution or discrimination. That is how Zionism began. What Herzl wanted when he created the Zionist movement was something like the French Third Republic, a bourgeois democracy. He didn't want to go beyond that. If you look at his book the *Judenstaat* (The State of the Jews), you will see that he speaks of a constitution which is similar to that of a European bourgeois democracy. Of course, you can say that Herzl was temperamentally a romantic nationalist, with a messianic mission, but his doctrine was liberal. My friend Dr. Weizmann, who was the first president of Israel, was not in that sense a nationalist. One can be a patriot without being a nationalist.

R. J.   We will come back to Weizmann later. Can we continue on Herder? You consider Herder as the first anti-colonial and anti-imperialist thinker. As a matter of fact, you find a real affinity between him and Karl Marx.

I. B.   Only in that respect. But I don't think that Herder is the first anti-colonial thinker in history. There was in France a *Société des Amis des Noirs*[1]. Well, that had a humani-

1. Founded by Brissot in 1788, its aim was to prepare for the emancipation of the Blacks. It was supported by such men as Condorcet and L'Abbé Grégoire.

tarian mission. But it was different for Herder and Marx. For Marx, the non-European colonial peoples were not really adult human beings: they were victims of capitalist imperialism. He thought of them entirely in terms of people whose national revolts might be of use to the Revolution, as in India or Ireland. But he never thought, as far as I know, that they would have states of their own, republics, parliaments, etc. But Herder believed in independent liberated nations. He believed that colonial nations must be able to create their own cultural identities. But for Marx, culture is Western. There is no evidence that Marx thought of any real culture outside the West—China was remoter from his mind than from Voltaire's.

R. J.   Why do you think that Herder was so fascinated by the survival of the Jews?

I. B.   Partly because he was a clergyman and he knew Hebrew, and he knew Hebrew poetry. One of his earliest works is on Hebrew poetry. Secondly, because he was interested in the self-expression of national groups before centralization crushed individual cultures as has been done by Alexander the Great and Rome and the barbarians. Now, the Jews are typical for Herder of a remarkably fertile native culture which managed to survive. That's why he says that we have to understand how these Judaeans lived and felt and thought, to understand the Bible which was their national epic. If you had not seen rough sailors struggling in the tempest on the sea, you could not understand the Norse and Finnish primitive poetry, which he thought magnificent. That is why Herder is interested in the Jews, and he wants every little cultural entity to survive and develop and not be crushed. Herder says that when you take the seeds buried with the mummies in the ancient Egyptian coffins and replant them after 3000 years, they give flowers; if you replant the Jews in Palestine there will be a nation again.

This is not sympathy for German Jews like Mendelssohn who believed in some form of integration, but it's the belief that the Jews have their own contribution, which they cannot make if they are absorbed by other cultures. Jews are Jews, not Germans. German Jews were, I expect, offended by Herder.

R. J.   And yet, Herder blames the Jews for not preserving a sufficient sense of collective honour.

I. B.   Yes, he blames the Jews for not going back to Palestine.

R. J.   Why do you consider Herder an empiricist?

I. B.   Well, he was a Christian clergyman and so he believed in the Christian doctrine which is not empirical, but so far as he is concerned with history, he simply believes in careful observation. He simply wanted to learn what people were like: hence he believed that one has to learn their languages and read their books, and enter their fears, hopes, images, collective outlooks. This is a kind of empiricism. It is not *a priori* like Hegel. You remember Hegel knew *a priori* that every nation makes its contribution to culture only once, and then gets off the stage. Well, he was wrong about China, and perhaps India too.

R. J.   For Herder, every group has a right to be happy in its own way; that's why he thinks that it's a terrible arrogance to affirm that everyone should become European. Do you agree with Herder on this point?

I. B.   Yes, why not? So long as they don't fight each other and are not aggressive, why shouldn't you allow people to develop their own culture in their own way? Let us take the Black problem in America: integration and autonomy for

105

the Blacks are terrible problems. It is the same thing with coloured people in England. I mean in theory we ought to have peaceful, well-integrated, multi-cultural societies, but clearly it's not something that is easily achieved.

R. J.   Do you think also that it's a terrible arrogance to affirm in today's world that everyone should become modern?

I. B.   Well, that doesn't have to be so, but if people want to defend themselves against exploitation, they must develop a strong economic base of their own. I don't think that new technologies are something that people need at every phase of history. But what mind can achieve, it should. If you can produce food more cheaply, you should. The idea of setting the clock back has always been a disaster. Take for example Bakunin. He wanted to abolish universities, because he thought that university graduates would be made too uppish by education, and he wanted total equality. He didn't want people to look down on workers and peasants. So he thought of abolishing institutions which promote intellectual inequality. Herzen was more intelligent than Bakunin and he said: "You cannot stop scientific progress. It's not weapons that create damage, it's their users." You can't stop the march of mind, all you can do is to prevent it from being misused. But the idea of liquidating the corrupt society, and then purifying everything before going forward is what in 1968 excited the students. They wanted first to eliminate all that was evil—destroy the old world—and then go forward. This is neither possible nor desirable. Utopia only ends in bitterness and frustration.

EIGHTEENTH-CENTURY RELATIVISM

R. J.   Do you agree with Herder's relativism?

I. B.   I don't think he was a relativist. I don't think there are relativists in the eighteenth century. I have written a piece on the absence of relativism in the eighteenth century.

R. J.   Well, in your essay on Montesquieu you speak of him as a relativist.

I. B.   If I did, I was mistaken. He only says that Persians do one thing and French do another. In a paper which I read in Pisa on the attribution of relativism to eighteenth-century thought, I explain my position. Different cultures have different ideals. Relativism means you like coffee with sugar, I like it without. There is no way of establishing which is right, tastes differ, values differ. One of the objections to that is that this proposition itself cannot be asserted as objective. Relativism can't be stated, because the proposition which expounds relativism cannot itself be relative. You claim absolute truth for it. So, different cultures have different ideals. These ideals are ultimate values for these cultures. They are not the same. But if I have enough cultural empathy, if I understand, as Herder wants me to do, what the centre of gravity of a culture is, then I understand why people in those circumstances pursue the goals they do. More than that, I can understand how I myself in those circumstances could have pursued it or could have rejected it; it is one of the lasting human goals, not outside the horizon of normal men. That is what pluralism is. Relativism says: "The Nazis believe in concentration camps and we don't" and there is no more to say. But I wish to say: "If I understand why the French in the eighteenth century believed in classical doctrines and the Germans preferred Hebrew literature or Shakespeare as objectively more desirable, I can understand both." I may prefer my ideals. The fact that they might not survive is not the reason for not fighting for them. Schumpeter rightly said that people who believe that ideals have to be absolute, are idolatrous barbarians. Civilization means that you must allow the possibility of change without ceasing to be totally dedicated to—and ready to die for—your ideals so long as you believe in them. Plato and Aristotle believed that men naturally lived in a public world—participated, at whatever level, in the life of the city. Their successors, Stoics, Epicureans, Cynics, Sceptics, did not: they advocated a quest for individual self-perfection. The Roman Stoics tried to combine them. But of course all sides understood each other's ideals, even if they were critical of them. These ideals all fell within the moral spectrum of rational beings: a Stoic can enter the mind of a Platonist and understand how one might pursue Platonic goals, without accepting them himself; those ideals, goals, ways of life are not subjective: they belong to the constellation of values in terms of which we can communicate with people whose forms of life may be different from ours—living in different conditions at different times. Relativists, Spenglerians, Positivists, deconstructionists are wrong: communication is possible between individuals, groups, cultures, because the values of men are not infinitely many; they belong to a common horizon—the objective, often incompatible, values of mankind—between which it is necessary, often painfully, to choose.

MORALITY AND RELIGION

R. J.   But you believe in universal moral rules?

I. B.   Yes, in a sense: I believe in moral rules which a great many people, in a great many countries, for a very long time have lived by. This acceptance makes it possible to live together. But if you say "absolute rules", then I have to ask you "What makes them so?", and "founded on what?" that returns to the *a priori* again. If you mean by universal an intuitive certainty of these rules, I think that I do feel a kind of an intuitive certainty, but if you tell me that somebody else has a quite different outlook, set of intuitions, I can, unless they are unintelligible, with an effort, grasp how someone might come to have such values although I may have to protect myself from such a culture if it endangers my own. I believe that in fact human beings, and their outlooks, are much more similar than Herder believed, and that cultures resemble each other far more than e.g. Spengler or even Toynbee asserted. But still they do differ, and may be irreconcilable. But I am quite clear that I do not have the faculty which detects absolute moral rules. Somebody like Leo Strauss believes in them because he believes in a faculty which some call "reason". "*La raison a toujours raison*," said somebody during the French Revolution, and Strauss's reason detects absolute values. I envy him. I just don't happen to have that kind of *raison*. I don't know if you have it. Some faculty which gives infallible truth in answer to central questions of life.

R. J.   But in Kantian terms one can speak of universal moral rules.

I. B.   Yes, but Kant does not give a convincing explanation of how we come to know what is right and what is wrong. We know it of course, because we live by a moral code: some call it conscience—we—the vast majority of mankind—live in the light of what we normally regard as unbreakable principles. But for Kant this is not an empirical proposition: moral law is revealed by reason; it works outside the empirical realm, the realm of sense perception, it is a special "noumenal" faculty which tells you nothing about the world we live in, but reveals truth about God, soul and immortality—that is Kant's phrase. The nature of this faculty seems to me, as it has to so many others, difficult to comprehend. Kant was a Christian and, indeed, a pietist; I think that it is this that leads him to postulate a transcendent world. I have myself no sense of a reality above and beyond the life I know. I am not religious, but I place high value on the religious experience of believers. I am moved by religious services—those of the synagogue, but also of churches and mosques. I think that those who do not understand what it is to be religious, do not understand what human beings live by. That is why dry atheists seem to me blind and deaf to some forms of profound human experience, perhaps the inner life: it is like being aesthetically blind. Mere capacity for feeling is not enough to enable one to understand other human beings, believers, unbelievers, mystics, children, poets, artists. Reason and experience are not enough. When you are profoundly moved by a work of art, it is difficult to say that it is an empirical experience. Every experience is, of course, in a sense empirical, but this is not something which you can subject to verification or experiment. You can't say it is true or false, real or unreal, you can only say it is sublime, upsetting, beautiful, profound or shallow. If you ask me what "profound" means, I am unable to tell you. There are all kinds of words which we use, which we know the meaning of, but we cannot explain. Take for example the word "profound". Why do we say that Pascal is a profounder thinker than Russell, Wittgenstein than Ayer? Because they touch a nerve and thereby reveal sometimes quite suddenly something which is part of our common experience and matters very greatly in our lives, but of which we were not clearly aware. Even Hume was not an atheist. The *Dialogues Concerning Natural Religion* simply say that the arguments for the existence of miracles are weaker than the arguments against it. Hume was an agnostic. You know that when he was in Paris he went to a dinner given by Baron d'Holbach. He asked him: "Are there any atheists in Paris?" and Holbach said: "There are twenty-three of them (or whatever number Holbach mentioned) sitting round you now." Hume was deeply shocked, or at least astounded.

HUME AND BRITISH PHILOSOPHY

R. J.   Now that we have got to this point, let us speak of your essay, "Hume and the Sources of German Anti-Rationalism". Do you think that Hume was a more destructive critic than Kant of the old rationalism?

I. B.   Yes, I think he was. Because he believed in custom, the belief of sensible men of all ages, but not in indubitable general propositions. He was politically a conservative, a Tory, not a Whig. He did not believe in absolute doctrines: he was anti-Cromwell, and no more than Burke believed in *a priori* principles. He was a bold, highly original philosopher. His epistemology is faulty: his atomism, his theories of perception, of memory, of imagination, seem to me invalid. But on political and ethical matters I think he said important and courageous things.

R. J.   Is that why the German opponent of the Enlightenment like Hamann turned to Hume to establish their position?

I. B.   Yes. Hume was useful for people like Hamann, even if he hated Hume.

R. J.   Why did Hamann hate Hume?

I. B.   Because he was an empiricist and a *philosophe*. Hume didn't believe in mystical revelation, he didn't believe in Hamann's world, where every event is a miracle, and where God speaks to us through the Bible, through Nature, through history, but he did think that even heretics and wicked people could be of use, because they can say some true things which one could use. He borrowed Hume's weapons, his anti-metaphysical views—against Hume's allies. Hume said that he could not *prove* the existence of a

111

material object: only believe it, however unavoidably. Hamann unargued—belief, faith, if about a table, why not in God?

R. J.   How is it that British philosophy is much more influenced by Hume than by Locke for example?

I. B.   Well, it is influenced by Locke too. Why do you think the British philosophers are not interested by Locke?

R. J.   Maybe because they refer more to Hume's philosophy than to Locke's.

I. B.   No. British philosophy is in general an empirical philosophy which begins with Bacon. From Bacon it moves to Hobbes and to Locke. Locke is an empiricist, not in matters of religion and ethics, but certainly in matters of knowledge of world and nature. Then comes Berkeley who certainly believed in God and in certain forms of non-empirical experience. But again, about what might be called the external world he is an empiricist, so are Hume, and J. S. Mill. Then there is a Hegelian reaction. After that comes Bertrand Russell, an original philosopher who rebelled against his own early Hegelianism. He was converted by G. E. Moore who is the beginning of the neo-empiricism. Moore did not start by refuting the Hegelians. He simply said, "Before you begin building these great systems, let us make sure what the bricks are made of." By this very minute examination, he reaches the conclusion that all these grand propositions don't have very firm foundations. Moore was an acute and totally honest thinker and converted Russell to the belief that what we see and hear and touch and smell and taste, must, in the end, be the basis of all we know of the external world.

R. J.   So you don't think that Hume is at the centre of British philosophy?

I. B.   Yes, but so are Locke, and Berkeley. There are differences. But they all represent various types of empiricism.

R. J.   Let's go back to the problem of "reason", which you said you didn't believe in.

I. B.   I never said that I didn't believe in "reason". But I simply don't understand what some philosophers mean by reason, which is for them a kind of a magical eye, which sees non-empirical universal truths.

R. J.   You mean those people who believe in a rational method of justifying norms and values?

I. B.   Not even justifying, but those who believe in an immediate perception of the eternal truth of certain norms.

R. J.   But how can one ground norms and values if he or she doesn't believe in the rational method of justifying them?

I. B.   You don't justify them. The norms don't need justification, it is they which justify the rest, because they are basic. The question is: "How do you reach these norms?" Well, there are all sorts of norms. One just finds that one's form of life presupposes certain concepts, categories and beliefs. That's a "de facto" statement, not "de jure". You can say that every civilization distinguishes between good and bad, between true and false. From that it does follow that this is virtually a universal fact about mankind; but not an *a priori* form of rational knowledge.

THE RIGHTS OF MAN

R. J.   But what are the grounds for preferring democracy to any other kind of regime?

I. B.   Because it is based on belief in human rights.

R. J.   Well, that's universal.

I. B.   Of course; but it isn't based on rational insights. If you ask why we believe in human rights, I can say because that is the only decent, even tolerable way human beings can live with each other, and if you ask what is "decent", I can say that is the only kind of life which we think that human beings should follow, if they are not to destroy each other. These are general truths, but this does not assume something unalterable. I can not guarantee anything against change.

R. J.   But when you talk about human rights, you talk about natural rights, which is an *a priori*.

I. B.   Of course, and that's why I deny it.

R. J.   But you don't deny human rights?

I. B.   No, I deny *a priori* lists of natural rights. I believe passionately in human rights; this follows from a great deal else that we all accept, but it is not demonstrable *a priori*. Of course, I don't deny that there are general principles of behaviour and human activity without which there cannot be a minimally decent society. Don't ask me what I mean by decent. By decent I mean decent—we all know what that is. But if you tell me that one day we will have a different culture, I can't prove the contrary.

R. J.   Therefore, you think that no political philosophy can get close to such a thing as "perfect reason"?

I. B.   I don't think there is such a thing as a direct non-empirical knowledge, intuition, inspection of eternal principles. Only universal human beliefs.

VERDI, STRAVINSKY, WAGNER

R. J.   Now let us speak of Verdi: you wrote about him in your book *Against the Current*[2].

I. B.   Let me just tell you that Verdi was not "against the current". So, it was maybe wrong to put him in that particular collection.

R. J.   Maybe he is not against the current, but you do consider him as a typical Herderian musician?

I. B.   No. He was an Italian nationalist. He believed in Mazzini. He believed in the Italian Risorgimento. He believed that the Italians should not be governed by the Austrians. His opera *Nabucco* is directed against the Austrians.

R. J.   Is that why you think that one should know Verdi's political views to be able to understand his music?

I. B.   Well, it helps to understand the spirit of some of his operas. I don't believe just in listening to tunes. I think one must understand the central concept of a work of art, not only to enjoy it, but also if you want to understand what the composer wants to convey. Let us take for example *Rigoletto*. At the centre of *Rigoletto* lie two ideas: one is Father and Daughter, a central relationship, the other is disgust with arbitrary and cruel renaissance princes: Hugo's play is a denunciation of the loathsome regimes and dissolute tyrants who trample on their subjects' rights. So the two fundamental ideas of *Rigoletto* are: republicanism and humanism. If you don't understand that, then I think *Rigoletto* is simply a succession of musical sounds. That's why I think that when

2.   "The 'Naiveté' of Verdi" (1968), reprinted in *Against the Current*.

Rigoletto was translated, as it was by the director Jonathan Miller, a very gifted man, into a story about the Mafia in New York, I did not quite like that, because for one mafioso to seduce the daughter of another mafioso is quite different from the Duke of Mantua seducing the daughter of a miserable jester, one has a social implication, the other doesn't. Verdi was extremely conscious of social injustice.

R. J.   In what sense is Verdi naive?

I. B.   In Schiller's sense. Schiller distinguishes the *naiv* —and the *sentimentalisch*: *sentimentalisch* doesn't mean sentimental. He distinguished between artists who create naturally, who are not troubled by the burden of the tragic disorder of life, who do not seek salvation in art as some people seek personal salvation in religion or Socialism or nationalism. Verdi in that sense is simply a craftsman of genius with the simple strong moral ideas of his time and place—no tragic self-torment. He was a marvellous composer, a divine genius who created in a natural way as Homer and Shakespeare and perhaps Goethe did.

R. J.   Why do you think that Verdi was the last naive composer in the history of music?

I. B.   I said he was, but I don't think that is true. The last naive composer is perhaps Bruckner. And what about jazz musicians? They are probably quite naive but I find jazz unbearable, so I can't talk about them. Jazz is not music to me. When Schiller speaks of *naiv*, he means that the work of art conceals the artist. When the artist is completely at one with his work, you don't need to know about his life to understand his work, everything is said by the work itself. This is not true of the *sentimentalisch* artists—Baudelaire, Mahler, Wagner, Rimbaud.

R. J.   How is it that you are more fascinated by Verdi than by the Russian composers?

I. B.   Because he is a greater composer. I think Verdi is a great composer, who wrote about primary human passions, in primary colours. There are not many great Russian composers. There are three truly great Russian composers: one is Mussorgsky, one is Tchaikovsky and the third is Stravinsky. Can you think of anybody else? Glinka? Rimsky-Korsakov? Borodin? Surely not.

R. J.   Yes, Prokofiev and Shostakovitch.

I. B.   No. They are excellent, but not of the order of Stravinsky, as Donizetti and Bellini are not on a par with Verdi. Stravinsky was a pure genius, a very original composer.

R. J.   Did you know him?

I. B.   Yes, I knew him quite well. Somebody introduced us and we got on quite well. He used to come to London to give concerts, and I saw him then. We met in New York and in Venice, and he came once or twice to Oxford to see us. Schoenberg and Stravinsky dominated modern music. The strange thing is that they lived within about thirty miles from each other in Beverly Hills but they never met. That was surely deliberate.

R. J.   So you do appreciate contemporary music and composers like Berg and Webern?

I. B.   Certainly.

R. J.   How about German classical composers like Wagner, Mahler?

I. B.   We can even go back to the beginning and speak of Bach. But it is simply impossible to compare these people. Bach is like one's daily bread, absolutely basic. One can never get tired of bread. I cannot conceive of being tired of hearing Bach; while one can—seldom, but still—get surfeited with listening to Mozart. But you cannot say Bach is greater than Mozart or Mozart is greater than Beethoven. These are foolish questions; the greatest creative artists are not commensurable. Schubert is for me one of the greatest composers. The wonderful pianist Alfred Brendel, who is a friend of mine, made me understand what Schubert conveys: particularly the tragic in his works.

R. J.   So, you are fascinated by the German composers?

I. B.   Of course, I consider Wagner to be a composer of genius. I have now heard the *Ring* four times. It is a fantastic achievement, even if I do not find it sympathetic. If you tell me that I shall never be able to hear Wagner again, I would not be miserable. But I see Wagner as a phenomenon of the first order in European culture, and not just in music. After Wagner nothing in the West was ever the same.

R. J.   Do you consider him an anti-Semite?

I. B.   Of course. He happened to have a nasty nature, but that is irrelevant to the value of his art. The point is that he changed Western music. Music could not be written after Wagner as it had been before him. He thoroughly affected the other arts. *La revue wagnerienne* was not particularly about music but about the new values in literature and all the arts. There are figures like Rousseau, Marx, Wagner, who change things radically, for good or ill; usually both. These are major personalities whom you cannot not recognize as epoch-making forces in the history of human culture.

118

MOSES HESS: ZIONIST

R. J.   You also consider Moses Hess to be a "naive". Do you use the word "naive" for Hess in the same way as for Verdi?

I. B.   Moses Hess is a naive in the ordinary sense, not in Schiller's sense. He was a good, kind and noble man of complete integrity but perhaps too simple. People like Marx and Engels mocked him. They liked him, but were ironical about him. He was an utterly decent man, and never said what he did not believe to be true. He said this even though it went against what he wanted to believe. That's why I think he was a very honourable man.

R. J.   Why were you interested in Moses Hess?

I. B.   Because he is the founder of Zionism, not because of his Hegelian views, which are quite interesting, but he is not a major figure in the history of Hegelian ideas.

R. J.   He seems very close to Herder?

I. B.   He wrote a famous book, *Rome and Jerusalem*, that nobody read, particularly prominent German Jews; but one did review it and told Hess he was talking nonsense. He told German Jews things they did not like. For example, he said something like this (I quote from distant memory): "Why don't Germans like you? It is not because they do not like your religion, or your writings or your economic behaviour. What they really do not like are your noses, your curly hair, because they think that they are not German, which you claim to be. And this you cannot change." Something on these lines. Heine earlier had said much the same.

R. J.   You consider *Rome and Jerusalem* a masterpiece?

I. B.   Well, it is. It is full of Hegelian language. Hess was brought up on Hegel and he was a tremendous admirer of Karl Marx. He was a Communist and a liberal nationalist, on Mazzinian lines, to the end of his life, a mysterious mixture. But he was a man who for the first time understood the Herderian principle that people can only create if they are independent and they can only be independent if they have a land of their own. They don't need a particular political organization, a homeland is enough.

R. J.   But the Hegelian language is still very relevant and many philosophers continue to write in this style.

I. B.   Who for example?

R. J.   Well I think of Kojève.

I. B.   Yes, but Kojève never really wrote much. He wrote letters to Leo Strauss. His famous book *Introduction à la Lecture de Hegel* are notes taken down by Raymond Queneau. When I asked Kojève if he wanted to add anything to the book, he said: "I didn't write this book, people put it down. I have nothing against it, but I have nothing to do with it." He took a very ironical attitude toward it. You know Kojève had a certain dandyish quality. He flirted with ideas, brilliantly.

R. J.   Do you consider that the Hegelian language is antiquated?

I. B.   No. But it is no good to me. I am a product of British empiricism. I am too old to change. Herder writes clearly, Kant wrote very clearly in his earlier days: but then came *The Critique of Pure Reason*. The ideas are of great originality and depth, but the apparatus of technical terms led to the tangled forests of later German philosophical prose; this ruined philosophical language in Germany, although Kant certainly tried to write clearly. After Hegel, German philosophers and French philosophers after the Second World War abandoned prose intended to be generally understood—used from the pre-Socratics to early Kant—and wrote as from under water, darkly, though there were exceptions—among materialists, Bergsonians, positivists, a few phenomenologists—all the thinkers proscribed under Lenin.

R. J.   How about Schopenhauer and Nietzsche?

I. B.   Schopenhauer is beautifully clear, but he hated Hegel, and escaped his influence. So did Nietzsche. But then neither of them were academics.

R. J.   Let us go back to Moses Hess.

I. B.   You know, he never called himself Moses Hess. He never signed himself Moses. He called himself Moritz Hess. He was called Moses Hess after his death. *Rome and Jerusalem* was not written by Moses Hess, but by M. Hess.

R. J.   In your essay on Moses Hess, you consider him to be very much concerned by the problem of nationalism as a true pre-condition of internationalism and you make a distinction between him on one side, and Marx and Disraeli on the other.

I. B.   Not Disraeli, only Marx. Hess believed, as did Mazzini, that true internationalism must be based on mutual regard and respect between nations. To have internationalism you must have individual nations. Whereas Marx looked on mankind, especially the working class, as one single body, Hess and Herder believed in individual nations which could and should have close relations with each other, but could each preserve its national identity and its national individuality. Marx took no interest in this. He saw mankind as divided solely into workers and capitalists and their agents and allies. There is another thing which separates both Marx and Disraeli from Hess, and that is their relation to their Jewish origins. Marx and Disraeli were both troubled by it. Marx suppressed it, Disraeli returned to it, almost obsessively, all the time. But Hess felt quite comfortable about it. He denounced the rich Jews in his early writings, but he never felt uncomfortable about the so-called Jewish problem. In the famous Damascus case, of—I think—1840, when Jews were accused of killing a monk to use his blood for ritual purposes—a great scandal in its day which the Church tried to ignore—he reacted as a Jew. At about this time he felt excited by Becker's German patriotic song against the French (*Sie werden ihn nicht haben, den guten deutschen Rhein*), and wrote music for it, and sent it to the poet who returned his score with the words scribbled on it "You are a Jew." He never forgot this and this—Damascus—may have started him off on his later Zionism.

R. J.   Why is Hess so much despised by Marx?

I. B.   For many reasons. First, because he did not greatly respect his intellect; because he was idealistic and believed in the possibility of peaceful transition to Communism, against what Marx supposed to be inevitable class war—or violent conflict. Marx did not much like disciples who did not completely accept every word he uttered. As far as I know, Marx never admitted any valid criticism of his mistakes. Hess remained touchingly loyal to him, so that when he died, Marx wrote quite a nice letter of condolence to his wife and praised his personal character. Marx never hated Hess as, for example, he hated Lassalle. Lassalle was a rival, who created the German Workers' Party, without which Socialism would not have developed as a force and that Marx couldn't swallow.

MARX AND THE NINETEENTH-CENTURY
SOCIALIST MOVEMENT

R. J. In your book on Karl Marx, you consider him an unsentimental person, who took no interest in persons or in states of minds.

I. B. Marx was unsentimental; at certain moments Marx showed emotion, but they are not frequent. In one of his letters to Engels, he tells him about his deep misery after the death of his son: Engels urges certain psychological remedies—Marx replies that this cannot help him—he is not one of these fortunate people, he cannot avoid suffering after a terrible loss. Marx was a hard-headed and hard-hearted man. He virtually liked only Engels, his own family and very few other people—Helene Demuth, Dr Kugelmann, Wilhelm Liebknecht, Charles (later Sir Charles, Professor of Fine Art in Cambridge University) Wallstein and perhaps a few English allies. Towards the end of his life, hardly anyone other than his wife and daughters.

R. J. Why did he dislike the fact that he was born a Jew?

I. B. Mainly because he identified the Jews with capitalism. Of course he was baptized as his father was, and regarded Judaism—like other religions—as passing phenomena, products or diseases of capitalism—which would vanish without a trace after the revolution. In his own world anti-Semites attacked him as a Jew—Bakunin, Ruge, Proudhon, Dühring—and other Leftists. Some degree of anti-Jewish feeling was quite normal throughout European society—and is perhaps so still, but Proudhon and Bakunin were really ferocious haters of the Jews.

R. J.   Why do you consider Marx an oddly isolated figure among the revolutionaries of his time?

I. B.   All I meant by that was that Marx was not a revolutionary in the sense of taking a personal part in revolutions of the day, like Bakunin, like Engels, like Proudhon. These people were active, but Marx remained outside revolutionary activity. He was a teacher, an ideologue. Of course he was a fighter, but he fought with words. He did not take up physical weapons or march in demonstrations; he could have done so in 1848, but he chose not to, Marx did not believe in direct action until the time was historically ripe. Not the cause but history alone was the guide.

R. J.   Marx owed much to Hegel. Do you think Marxist philosophy could have existed without the influence of Hegel and German philosophy?

I. B.   Not in the form it took. The idea of dialectic, a spiritual movement, means everything to Hegel; Marx used it, but translated into material terms—which is something very different, and to me, very unclear. Marx was a thinker of genius and said important things. But his genius took the form of creating a synthesis of ideas which came from others. It is odd, but there is scarcely an idea in Marx which is not traceable to an earlier thinker. But the combination—the uniting doctrine—which he effects is a work of genius. You can similarly say of a symphony that it is a work of genius—although the notes can be heard elsewhere, the combination is new. Surplus value, class-war, the dominant historical role of changes in technology, base and super-structure, all this can be found elsewhere in Saint-Simon, Fourier, Hodgskin, Ricardo and so on; Marx was not a man who acknowledged debts to others. He did not say: "I owe this to Hegel, I owe that to Saint-Simon, or to Rodbertus or Helvétius or Lassalle", although he did. There is a famous Latin phrase which says: "*Pereant qui ante nos nostra dixerunt.*" It means: "Perish those who before us said what we are saying." Marx did not recognize sources as forerunners.

R. J.   You believe that Marx's intellectual system was a closed one, although he was not obsessed by fixed ideas.

I. B.   He was certainly obsessed by his own ideas. He never took anything back, once he thought of something, he believed that he made a contribution of eternal validity. Nor did he admit to modifying his views. But, as you know, the early Marx and the old Marx are not the same. The Marx of *Das Kapital* is not the same as the Marx of the *Philosophical and Economic Manuscripts* or of the *German Ideology*; nevertheless, there is never any attempt to say: "I developed, I had new ideas, what I said before was inadequate." Yet Marx, even if his ideas developed, was very much more single and solid than some people in France want to believe. I don't think there is an early humanistic Marx and a later economic Marx, a scientific Marx and a romantic Marx. People seem to me to have tried to think this, because they hate Stalinism, and want to rescue Marx from Stalin. But if you read Marx, the continuity in him and from him to Plekhanov, Lenin, Stalin is very clear.

R. J.   Do you consider Marx a relevant thinker?

I. B.   Certainly. Partly because his doctrines changed history, for better and for worse. And his analyses are often of great value. The world might have been a happier place, so some think, without Karl Marx, but he did exist and his ideas have entered the texture of modern thought even of those who are profoundly opposed to him.

THE LEFT AND THE SHIPWRECK OF MARXISM

R. J.   Do you think that Marxism is as alive today as it was twenty years ago?

I. B.   I think a very strange thing has happened. There obviously is something which can be described as left-wing thought; this, it seems to me, has collapsed in the West for the first time after more than two centuries. Let me clarify this proposition. The Left could be said to have begun, let us say, with Voltaire. Its centre is Paris. Voltaire is against the Church, against the *ancien régime*, against traditional values—considered by the authorities as a subversive figure. Voltaire's ideas were regarded in his day as dangerous to established orthodoxy. Then come the *philosophes* of the *Encyclopédie*. Then the great radical upheaval—the French Revolution. Then Bonapartism, a modification of radical ideas, but not a return to the Bourbons—there are certainly central radical elements in the Napoleonic organization of France—a rational legal code, little respect for royalty or for tradition in the first, Napoleonic Empire. Then comes the Restoration, but in the 1820s there still proliferate conspiracies in Paris against the regime. Babeuf is dead, but Buonarroti is at work. This is followed by radical German workers' circles in France, and *La Société de Quatre Saisons*, and left-wing Carbonari. In the 1840s Paris is full of revolutionaries—Bakunin, Marx, Herzen, Louis Blanc, Proudhon, Dézamy, Blanqui, Leroux, George Sand's other socialist friends—Saint-Simonians, Fourierists, Socialists, Communists, anarchists. Then 1848, and after that Napoleon III, and suppression of radical action. But Victor Hugo and Michelet became identified with the republican forces which are against the Empire and they write and agitate and leave France in protest, so do the exiles in London for twenty years. Then the Commune, and after the Commune, Socialist parties, Marxists, Allemanists, Possibilists, Jaurès, Guesde,

126

Dreyfusards etc. Then the radical governments which dissolve the monasteries. Then, after the First World War, the Third International, and the majority of French Socialists cross over to the Communists. Paris remains the great centre of a variety of left-wing ideas, pro- and anti-Moscow. Then comes the Second World War, and the Communist Resistance, and then intellectuals like Sartre and Merleau-Ponty, who inspired some Asian and African revolutionaries, and so on. Then, finally the *événements* of 1968. After that, suddenly, silence. Let us take the case of a young man today. He wants to help the poor against the rich, he wants social justice and equality, the abolition of capitalism, he wants a decent human society with a rational organization. Who are his leaders today? Even if some of them might be charlatans, where are they? Who are the new charismatic leaders of the Left in Paris, the centre of Leftism, or anywhere else. Where is he to look? The Greens? The feminists? Is this all that remains of the old Left?

R. J.   Well, I believe there is no charismatic leader of the Left in today's France.

I. B.   All we have in England is the ageing E. P. Thompson who preaches nuclear disarmament, and Mr Tony Benn. Not much.

R. J.   Actually, the main left-wing movements in Europe today are anti-nuclear movements.

I. B.   They do not have a charismatic leader. Name me a left-wing leader whom the young can, rightly or wrongly, find inspiring? Cohn-Bendit, the late Dutschke, Hayden?

R. J.   How about Mitterrand in France?

I. B.   Mitterrand is very moderate. He is not terribly left-wing, is he? I don't think he is so much a Socialist, as a member of a gradualist Labour Party.

R. J.   What happened to the Labour Party?

I. B.   Two things happened. First, the Soviet Union has betrayed them. You know, in a way, even if they sharply condemned Stalin and all his works and crimes, their hope was in that direction. Socialism which has gone wrong but is still Socialism—a corrupt perverted workers' state, but a workers' state; Lenin saved the Revolution; Bukharin was an honest communist—Stalin and Beria are monsters and yet the Left looks hopefully to Socialist countries, even Israel. If Russia has betrayed the ideal, then Yugoslavia is better. If no longer Yugoslavia, then China. Later Cuba, Nicaragua. But basically the phenomenon of Communism in power has been discredited. Secondly, let me put it to you that the first purpose of Socialism, apart from social justice, is to give food to the hungry and to clothe the naked. No Socialist government has yet succeeded in doing that; Socialist economics have not delivered. Capitalism may be wicked, it may be oppressive, it may be exploitative, it may be commercializing and vulgarizing culture and destroying moral values, but there is more freedom in it, more variety, more self-expression. I do not believe that in the Soviet Union today there are truly believing Marxists—at most, very, very few. In England yes, in France, yes, and many in Latin America. But in Eastern Europe? The home of it all? Something has collapsed. There is a world shift to the Right. I wish it were not so. I am a liberal.

R. J.   What do you think of Gorbachov and Perestroika?

I. B.   I have no particular theory about him. I wish him well. When I went to the Soviet Union I talked to people all of whom were in favour of Perestroika, but most of whom were sceptical about the success of these reforms. There are still too many problems.

R. J.   What kind of problems?

I. B.   Mostly bureaucratic and economic problems. There was a terrible decline of economic life under Stalin. The workers are not well trained, not ingenious, not energetic or competent enough. Technologically they lag too far behind the West. The peasants are still primitive. The intelligentsia is excited, hopeful and morally attractive and critical. But there is a huge bureaucracy frightened of losing its power. There always has been a rigid, reactionary, and not very efficient, bureaucracy in Russia, a powerful army and a powerful secret police. But Gorbachov's first and greatest task is to rescue the economy—very, very, very difficult indeed. Even Brecht who was a Stalinist once said: "First fill one's belly, morality comes after." That is a defence of Stalinism, but under Stalin both eating and morality collapsed, there was starvation plus vicious extermination. Gorbachov has huge problems to face. I hope he succeeds.

R. J.   The Soviet intellectuals also have a lot of hope.

I. B.   The ones I met are often heroic, always sensitive, decent, gifted, exceptionally admirable people. Hope and despair alternate among them. Some of the young seem to me very civilized.

R. J.   How about people like Solzhenitsyn?

I. B.   I think Solzhenitsyn is rather like the Old Believers in the seventeenth century. They regarded Peter the Great as the devil on the throne. He thinks the Devil is Communism and it is a terrible curse whether in Russia or China and must be razed to the ground: all human values, especially the

129

traditional Russian ones, are trampled down by it—it must be eradicated.

R. J.   You don't agree with him?

I. B.   No. I think Communism is a total failure, and there are more terrible crimes on its conscience—if it exists—than on that of any other movement in history, even of the great religious persecutions. When I was in the Soviet Union in 1988 there was an article in one of the official journals, not in *samizdat*, but some official journal the name of which escapes me, which said that in the West they calculate that the number of the victims of Stalin is about fifteen to twenty million; but that is not correct—it is fifty million. Well, after that I do not see how one can begin to defend anybody inspired by this regime. I don't agree with the *nouveaux philosophes* in France, when they say Karl Marx leads directly to the Gulag. Karl Marx liked violence and violence breeds violence. Still, Karl Marx did not advocate mass murder— this is a new idea in the West. The true author of this is Lenin. Under Lenin more innocent people were extermi- nated than in any previous revolution, many more than in 1793 or 1848 or 1870. There was real terror, not on the scale of Stalin, but real terror which hit out right and left, it was on this that Leninism was based.

R. J.   But putting aside the failure of Communism as a political regime, it seems to me that Marxism as a form of philosophical thought has collapsed in the West.

I. B.   No, I think there are ideas you could find in Marx which belong to the general treasury of human ideas. For example, Marx was the first man to predict the rise of Big Business, to identify the influence of technology on general culture, to expose the springs of capitalist activity. He preached class war, and of course he exaggerated wildly—it is not a universal phenomenon and not as central or wide-spread as he thinks. There is no open, bitter, class war in England, or France or America, whatever the social tensions and injustices. Perhaps there is one in Nicaragua. China is a good example of the nightmares which fanatical Marxism can generate.

R. J.   Is that why you compare Marx to "an ancient prophet who performs a task imposed on him by Heaven"?

I. B.   Do I say that? No, I think that is an exaggeration. I think people said that just because his beard looked like those of Jewish prophets in Doré's Bible.

R. J.   Marx seems to be very much influenced by Judaism and by Christian thought.

I. B.   Possibly. Who was not in those days? They all read the Bible.

R. J.   But, what do you consider to be really new in Marx?

I. B.   As I've just said—his idea that changes in technology have a dominant influence on culture. That's a new idea. Saint-Simon said it, but few read Saint-Simon. What I mean is that the idea that art and culture are influenced by techno-logical change is a Marxist idea. Marxism in that sense is not dead; even though more of its doctrine—for example, its analysis of nationalism, religion, of the role of great leaders —is largely fallacious. No one else predicted Big Business as he did. Ideals are sometimes disguised interests, though not as invariably as he supposed. The question about an idea, a movement, an activity—whom do they benefit? Who gains most from them whatever the motivation which creates them? These are not silly questions.

131

R. J.   Marxism seems to be still alive in Third World countries.

I. B.   Naturally, wherever there is oppression and poverty, any doctrine which says: "your masters are animated by the worst of motives, conscious and unconscious", and "if you do this and that you are bound to win—history—the future—is on your side"—has followers. When he predicts the inevitable victory of the oppressed class, because the stars in their courses are fighting for them, it must appeal to the oppressed class. Marx gives them inextinguishable hope. "Do not fear; organize and victory will be yours." Christians think that it will happen in the next world, but Marx says it will happen in this one. You've heard of the banner in Moscow on which is written "Proletarians of the world, forgive us!" and "We have been on a journey of seventy years into nothing." Don't you think that there has been a radical "mutation" of the Left?

R. J.   I think that this "mutation" is the result of the philosophical bankruptcy of Marxism.

I. B.   Not only philosophical, but mainly economic, social and political. Do you know of any leaders who could organize powerful Communist movements?

R. J.   But I think Communism has no more "*raison d'être*".

I. B.   Yet, it still has many devotees in the world and in Latin America, and probably in Asia too. But historically speaking a major *bouleversement*—or mutation—has happened that nobody has fully described.

❖

A Philosophy
of Freedom

STEPHEN SPENDER: SIXTY YEARS
OF FRIENDSHIP

RAMIN JAHANBEGLOO I was reading today the auto-
biography of your friend Stephen Spender, *World within
World*, and there was a passage on you. I quote: "Isaiah
Berlin had an interest in people's lives which was strength-
ened by the conviction that he himself was detached from
the passions which moved them. Human behaviour was for
him a subject of fascinated enquiring." Is it still so?

ISAIAH BERLIN No. I don't think this was ever wholly
true. In the 1930s I lived in a college like a monk, I didn't
live much in the wider world. I observed my contemporaries in all kinds of emotional situations. I never thought I
was completely immune from them and later life confirmed
this.

R. J. Stephen Spender says also: "Berlin excelled in
description of people by metaphor." Is that true?

I. B. It could be. I can't tell you if it is true or not.

R. J. According to Spender, you both shared a great
passion for music, and for this reason you both went to
Salzburg?

I. B.   Yes. We both had—and still have—a passionate love of music.

R. J.   He says you have a great passion for Beethoven's quartets, and specially for *Fidelio*.

I. B.   That is true of me but particularly true of him. The pianist Artur Schnabel made a deep impression on both of us. He did much to form our musical taste. He played in London in the 1930s and we went to all his concerts. Schnabel was a marvellous musician. His profound interpretation of Beethoven and Schubert transformed our vision of classical music.

R. J.   Do you play music yourself?

I. B.   No. I have a bad left arm, it's a birth injury, so I would never have been able to play musical instruments— the oboe or clarinet, perhaps, but I never tried.

THE AIMS OF PHILOSOPHY

R. J.   Now I would like to ask you a few questions on your essays published in *Concepts and Categories*. In your essay, "The Purpose of Philosophy" you claim that for you there is no universally accepted answer to the question: "What is the subject of philosophy?" Well, what is the purpose of philosophy for you?

I. B.   I think the purpose of philosophy is to try to answer very general questions, I mean questions of general importance for which no technique either empirical or logical can provide solutions. When you are puzzled, and do not know where to look for answers, that is the symptom of a philosophical question. If you wish to know what is the meaning

of words like good and evil, it is no use looking in
dictionaries or encyclopedias, or any other book of reference, nor does investigation or logical reasoning help. There
is a famous example given by the excellent philosopher
G. E. Moore which is often regarded as a piece of typical
British triviality, but it seemed to me a good observation.
He said: "Supposing you ask somebody, 'Where is the
image in the mirror?' and he answers 'It's in the mirror.'
Yes, but not in the sense that the glass is in the mirror. So he
becomes puzzled and says: 'It is behind the mirror.' But if
you look behind the mirror, there is nothing there. Then he
says: 'It is on the mirror.' Yes, but not 'on' in the sense that
you can stick a stamp on it." Where are mirror images or
the double image if you press your eyeballs? You don't
know what to answer. Are they in space? Not in a physical
space. It all turns on the use of "in". There is no problem for
ordinary people, only for those interested in words and
meanings. This kind of problem is not terribly profound.
But if you think that it is nonsense, that it is a question that
no serious person could bother about, then you are not
interested in philosophy. Or take time and space. Suppose a
child says to you, "I want to be Napoleon at the battle of
Wagram." You tell him, "It's impossible." "Why?" he asks.
"Because he is dead," and the child asks, "What difference
does that make?" And you say: "Well you know it's a long
time in the past. Napoleon's body has disintegrated. You
can't meet him." If the child is very clever, he will say to
you: "Suppose we collect all the atoms of his body together
again, could we then see Napoleon?" "Yes, that is in
principle possible only in practice not." The child says: "But
I want to see Napoleon at Wagram not now, but then—in
the past. Can I see him as he was? Not as reconstructed
now?" You tell him, "No, you cannot travel into the past."
"Why not?" A Positivist will tell you that the phrase
"travelling into the past" makes no sense, given the usual
sense of our words—that all we mean by time can be

translated into "before", "after" and "at the same time as". There is no such medium, indeed no such entity as "time" to travel in. To say there is is a misuse of language. But then the child ripostes: "If it is a question of language, why can't we change the language so that I could see Napoleon at Wagram?" Normally, these are kinds of questions which puzzle children. It is at this point that parents say, "Don't bother me with silly questions, go and climb a tree". These silly questions which children can ask, are often real questions which penetrate to the heart of things. And if you are interested in that kind of thing, which has no practical significance, but if you have real intellectual curiosity, then you realize that there is a problem here, and seek for a method of dealing with it. Again, suppose I say that I can't exist at two periods of time at once. Why not? Is it the nature of time or the nature of the word "time"? Are all metaphysical statements translatable into questions about the use of words? Are all philosophical questions in the end verbal? Are there no prevalent categories of actual human experience and not only of the way we use words? Are all questions about the nature of what there is always fully answerable, at least in principle?

R. J.   So, you think it is part of human nature to ask philosophical questions?

I. B.   Well, I think children often do. Sometimes it suddenly occurs to people to ask you: "Can you tell me why I should do my duty?" or "Why should anyone obey anyone?" The last is a central question of political philosophy. Well, we don't get the answer by looking it up in encyclopedias or dictionaries. There are many answers. Some people say, because this is what God has ordered. Because my nurse, parents, teachers say so. Others speak of the Social Contract. Yet others say, because it is the wish of the majority or because it promotes human welfare. People speak of the intuitive, Kantian certainty of certain truths. Many answers have been given. If you don't quite know how to establish beyond doubt which is the correct answer —there is no accepted technique for this—then you are engaged in doing philosophy.

R. J.   It's very interesting to know, how the first philosophical problem came to exist in a man's mind.

I. B.   Who can tell? Well, I think of the first chapter of Genesis, when Adam is told that there is a tree of knowledge and a tree of life, and he is forbidden to enjoy the fruit of both. That is a philosophical statement.

R. J.   Don't you think there is a relation between freedom and philosophical investigation? I mean that one cannot ask philosophical questions, if one is not free to think?

I. B.   Yes. And I am sure all men at all times have come to ask questions of a fundamentally philosophical character. Philosophical questions are by no means only products of complicated civilizations. Some very simple questions turn out to be philosophical.

R. J.   How is it that in today's world we ask no more philosophical questions?

I. B.   But we do. The questions I have talked about can be discussed in Oxford, Harvard, Stockholm, Calcutta today. They are not discussed in France, because French philosophers mostly think that questions which don't deal directly with deepest problems of life and society are somehow trivial. But the English philosophers and the American philosophers still think they are very serious. And the history of philosophy bears this out. They are in the central tradition of Western thought.

R. J. So you don't agree with the fact that philosophy is losing its value in our world?

I. B. Certainly not. In countries like France, Italy or Spain, philosophy is supposed to tell you what to seek after, how to live. I mean they tend to be philosophies of life, *Lebens-philosophien*. Kant, Hegel, William James, Bergson, were philosophers in both senses—asked both types of questions—but then philosophy took a swerve—Nietzsche, Sartre, and I suppose Heidegger (whom I cannot read) veered away from the main traditions of philosophical thought. I don't think anybody could say that the twentieth century has not produced major thinkers. Bertrand Russell was a major thinker. So were Husserl and Wittgenstein. I think that in theory of knowledge, logic and the philosophy of mind, twentieth-century philosophy is superior to the nineteenth. Far greater discoveries were made. I regard the twentieth century as one of the boom periods of philosophy.

R. J. So you are against the idea of "the end of philosophy"?

I. B. Absolutely. As long as men are alive, philosophy will not come to an end.

R. J. And what do you think is the special task of a philosopher today?

I. B. I don't think philosophers have a special task. The task of philosophers is to do philosophy. The task of philosophers is to think about questions which interest them and try to clarify them, and if possible answer them. Philosophy has no special task today. The very question is based on a misunderstanding of what the purpose of philosophy is. It's as if you ask me what is the task of art today, or what is the function of love today? If you ask me "What is the purpose of art?" I think art has no purpose. The purpose of art is to be art. In the same way, the purpose of love is love. The purpose of life is life . . .

R. J.   And the purpose of philosophy?

I. B.   The purpose of philosophy is philosophy. The purpose of philosophy is pursuit of philosophical truth.

R. J.   Speaking of truth, I remember that in your essay "Political Ideas in the Twentieth Century", you claim that the rise of totalitarian ideologies has led humanity to a novel concept of truth, which would hardly have been intelligible to previous centuries. Can you clarify this idea?

I. B.   What I meant was that in totalitarian countries, people, instead of answering questions, try to prevent questions from being asked. One way of preventing people from asking questions is by suppressing them. You give dogmatic answers, and if they don't accept them you silence them. You don't allow people to question rules or opinions or institutions—you eliminate the very habit of questioning as subversive.

R. J.   So, there can be no philosophy in totalitarian countries?

I. B.   Yes, there can be. But it's very narrow. For example, there has been work on logic in the Soviet Union, which was considered mathematics, because it was not safe to call it philosophy. There have been works on metaphysics in the Soviet Union, but they are very dogmatic and uncritical. Just bad philosophy. Perhaps this will change now. Philosophy needs Glasnost more than any discipline. But there is not much of a philosophical tradition in Russia, it is true.

R. J.   So, you distinguish between good philosophy and bad philosophy?

I. B.   All philosophers do that. Good and bad applies to every human endeavour.

PLURALISM AND DEMOCRACY

R. J.   Do you consider your own philosophy a practical one? I mean how can one develop your philosophical ideas into a workable political guideline?

I. B.   On politics I do have some ideas. I don't know if you saw my lecture for the Agnelli Foundation. For instance one of my convictions is that some moral, social and political values conflict. I cannot conceive of any world in which certain values can be reconciled. I believe, in other words, that some of the ultimate values by which men live cannot be reconciled or combined, not just for practical reasons, but in principle, conceptually. Nobody can be both a careful planner, and, at the same time, wholly spontaneous. You cannot combine full liberty with full equality—full liberty for the wolves cannot be combined with full liberty for the sheep. Justice and mercy, knowledge and happiness can collide. If that is true, then the idea of a perfect solution of human problems—of how to live—cannot be coherently conceived. It is not that such a perfect harmony cannot be created, because of practical difficulties, the very idea of it is conceptually incoherent. Utopian solutions are in principle incoherent and unimaginable. Such solutions want to combine the uncombinable. Certain human values cannot be combined, because they are incompatible with one another; so there have to be choices. Choices can be very painful. If you choose A, you are distressed to lose B. There is no avoiding choices between ultimate human values, ends in themselves. Choices can be agonizing, but unavoidable in any world we can conceive of. Incompatible values remain incompatible in them all. All we can do is to protect choices from being too agonizing and that means that what we need is a kind of system which permits pursuit of several values so that, so far as possible, there arises no situation which makes men do something which is contrary to their deepest moral convictions. In a liberal society of a pluralist kind there is no avoiding compromises; they are bound to be made: the very worst can be averted by trade-offs. So much for this, so much for that. How much equality, how much liberty? How much justice, how much mercy? How much kindness, how much truth? Knowledge and happiness cannot always be combined. A man who discovers that he has cancer is not made happy by his knowledge. Ignorance may make him less free, but at the same time happier. This means that the idea of some ultimate solution of all our problems is incoherent. Those who believe in the possibility of a perfect world are bound to think that no sacrifice for that can be too great. For attaining perfection no price can be too high. They believe that if blood must be shed to create the ideal society, let it be shed, no matter whose or how much. You have to break eggs to make this supreme omelette. But once people get into the habit of breaking eggs, they don't stop—the eggs are broken but the omelette is not made. All fanatical belief in the possibility of a final solution, no matter how reached, cannot but lead to suffering, misery, blood, terrible oppression.

R. J.   What possible support can your theory of pluralism give to the problem of democracy?

I. B.   Democracy can sometimes be oppressive to minorities and individuals. Democracy need not be pluralistic, it can be monistic, a democracy in which the majority does whatever it wants, no matter how cruel or unjust or irrational. In a democracy which allows for opposition there is always hope that one might convert the majority. But democracies can be intolerant. Democracy is not *ipso facto* pluralistic. I believe in a specifically pluralist democracy, which demands consultation and compromise, which recognizes the claims—rights—of groups and individuals which, except in situations of extreme crisis, is forbidden to reject democratic decisions. Benjamin Constant wrote very well about the tyranny of democracy under the Jacobins. Constant is a genuine liberal.

R. J.   But you seem to be very close to Tocqueville at the same time, when he warned that democracy might usher in an overmighty central government?

I. B.   Oh yes, of course. Tocqueville was a pessimistic thinker, but there is a great deal of good sense in him. He advocated devolution of power. Both Constant and Tocqueville were conscious of the horrors of the excesses of the French Revolution: the whole of political theory in the nineteenth century (if you want to be dogmatic) is an attempt to explain what went wrong with the French Revolution. All the doctrines are answers to that, and Tocqueville's is so very clearly. Tocqueville certainly understands the need for devolution, pluralism, flexibility, loose textures. Some states governed by individual despots have been more liberal than some extreme democracies. Prussians under Frederick the Great certainly enjoyed more liberty of thought and action than the citizens of the Soviet Union, which suppressed all opposition and criticism. Even the Athenian democracy was not exactly tolerant when they expelled Anaxagoras and killed Socrates. The French Revolutionary assembly was democratic, but it said that the Revolution had no need of scientists, and so they killed Lavoisier, and in effect Condorcet too.

EQUALITY AND LIBERTY

R. J.   Well, the major problem with the French Revolution is that it was carried out in the name of the two principles of liberty and equality and it led to Jacobin Terror. Now, do you think that equality and liberty could be reconciled?

I. B.   Of course they can to some degree be combined, but you cannot combine maximum forms of them. If you have maximum liberty, then the strong can destroy the weak, and if you have absolute equality, you cannot have absolute liberty, because you have to coerce the powerful—the pike—if they are not to devour the poor and meek—the carp.

R. J.   I am very interested by your essay "Equality", because there aren't many liberals who write on this subject.

I. B.   I know.

R. J.   What do you understand by "equality"?

I. B.   Well, that's a very general question. Equality is always specific. Let me give an instance, if you have ten children, and you want to give each a piece of cake, if you give one child two slices and the next child none, for no good reason, this offends against the principle of equality. That is what "unfair" means.

R. J.   But traditionally speaking, liberalism and equality are not combinable.

I. B.   Historically, all kinds of things happen and total equality means the suppression of the liberties of those who

145

are superior to others. You remember that the great anarchist Mikhail Bakunin, who believed in equality, wanted to suppress universities because they produced people who were intellectually superior, who might lord it over the others. There is the despotism of egalitarianism. In the early years of Soviet Union some orchestras decided to get rid of conductors because they opposed all authority. It ended in total artistic failure. Total liberty can be dreadful, total equality can be equally frightful.

R. J.   Why do you think that liberty has this peculiar paradoxical quality and could the separation of the two concepts of liberty move the paradox?

I. B.   I examined two concepts of liberty. But there are more than these. I was writing about political liberty, not liberty in general. I think liberty is something that everybody is thought to want, and so all good things are brought in under that label. People try to make liberty mean all the things they like, and that is too imprecise, it creates terrible confusions of thought.

R. J.   Is that why you separate the two concepts of liberty?

I. B.   People speak of economic liberty, social liberty, political liberty, moral liberty, metaphysical liberty and so on. The point is that these things are different from each other. In some ways they are similar, in other ways they differ. In the nineteenth century liberty meant mainly social and political liberty. In the twentieth century it has become more complex, because economic analysis has made things more complex, because our knowledge of history has developed, so nobody any longer knows what precisely the word liberty means; what is exactly the relation of liberty A to liberty B, to liberty C, to liberty D? There has been a great increase both of knowledge and of understanding and that has increased the difficulty of giving clear answers. I distinguish two concepts of liberty, because I think they are both elements in Western thought, and think they are different from each other. They are answers to different questions, and people confuse them. The perversion of each has led to bad consequences, but one of them has, it seems to me, historically been more cruelly perverted than the other. I think that positive liberty has been distorted more disastrously than negative liberty, but I do not deny that negative liberty has been perverted into a species of "laissez-faire" which has led to terrible injustices and sufferings. I admit that I was deeply influenced by the monstrous misuse of the word liberty in totalitarian countries. Totalitarian regimes declared that they were homes of true liberty. That seems to be a cruel caricature of the word, and I thought that something had to be said about that. This did not please my left-wing critics. But then everything I have written has usually been attacked from both sides, from the Right and from the Left, with equal vehemence.

R. J.   Yes, your essay "Two Concepts of Liberty" has been attacked by critics. So was your essay "Historical Inevitability". But what made you write that essay?

I. B.   I was invited to give a lecture in memory of Auguste Comte, endowed by the Positivist Church, and I thought I would give a lecture on historical determinism. It seems to me that once people say: "I am the agent of history—we should do this or that, because history demands it, because the class demands it, because the nation demands it, because the route we take is a kind of progressive *autostrada*, along which we are driven by history itself, so that anything which gets in the way, must be swept aside"; once you are in that kind of frame of mind, you tend to trample on human rights and values. There is a need to defend basic decency against this kind of passionate, often fanatical, faith.

R. J.   Is that why you think determinism and responsibility are incompatible?

I. B.   They are. If history causes you to act as you do, how can you be personally responsible? I think this is Nietzsche's *amor fati* where there is moral choice if you are on a moving stair the direction of which cannot be changed—and if you identify your reason and purpose and morality with this inexorable movement, what can be meant by responsibility? I believe that there are moments in history when individuals or groups can freely alter the direction of things. Not everything is predictable. Men are free agents within narrow limits. The limits exist, but within them, there is space for choice. Unless there is choice, there is no human action. Everything is behaviour. Let me give you an example. I think that if Churchill had not been the British Prime Minister in 1940, the Nazis might have conquered Europe, in which case the history of Europe would certainly have been even more different than it has been from that which Karl Marx had predicted. If Lenin had died or become debilitated in April 1917, there would have been no Bolshevik Revolution; possibly a civil war, Liberals and Socialists versus monarchists, but the Bolshevik regime could not have been constructed by any one but Lenin. Trotsky couldn't have done it, because he was a Jew and a Jewish dictator was scarcely conceivable. So there *are* turning points in history. At these turning points individuals sometimes swing the issue in one direction or the other.

R. J.   I think there is a close relationship between your idea of liberty and your idea of history.

I. B.   Well, although I am a pluralist, there is, I suppose, some unity in my thought. My ideas are, for the most part, related to each other. They are not all separate entities.

R. J.   And for you life would have no meaning if we had no freedom to make choices and goals.

I. B.   Yes, but remember there are limits. I think we are confined by the nature of things. We haven't much choice. Let us say one per cent. But that one per cent can make all the difference.

R. J.   When you speak of limits, do you think of laws?

I. B.   The laws of Nature, of course, the laws of physics, chemistry, geology, climate, everything Montesquieu talked about, not human laws. Human laws can be changed. I cannot obviously tell you in general what the limits are. If you describe what a given situation and conditions are likely to be—I can try to indicate the limiting factors.

R. J.   Let us go back for a moment to the concept of liberty. Do you think that there is a necessary relationship between liberty and citizenship? I mean, does one need to be a citizen to be free, as the Greeks thought?

I. B.   Yes, of course, unless you include the Stoics and later Anarchists who rejected the State and therefore citizenship as such. The Greeks believed in laws. Herodotus believed in "isonomia" which means equality before the law, so did the sixth-century tyrannicides. It means freedom from oppression, from arbitrary rule. I believe in that too. Unless there are general rules, people cannot be protected from either despotism or chaos. Total freedom from laws is total anarchy. But I also believe that liberty means the absence of obstacles; but, of course, there must be some controls, that is, obstacles. The word liberty to me means absence of obstacles, but I am not a disciple of Bakunin or Kropotkin, I do not preach anarchism. I think if there are no restraints,

149

there can be no peace, men will destroy each other. A man on an island—Robinson Crusoe—is totally free, until Man Friday arrives. After that reciprocal obligations begin—and there is the problem of enforcement. Kant was right, as so often. The bird may think that it would fly more freely in a vacuum: but it would not—it would fall. There is no society without some authority: and this limits liberty.

R. J.   So you are against Bakunin when he claims: "I only become truly free from the liberty of others"?

I. B.   Many people have said that. In a way it makes sense. It only means that if some people are not free, then the liberty of others is to some degree affected. In a slave society, the slave owners cannot develop themselves as free men so long as they have slaves, because it corrupts their lives, power does tend to corrupt. Lord Acton was right. Democratic freedom is not divisible.

R. J.   Do you agree with Charles Taylor when he characterizes negative liberty as the "opportunity concept"?

I. B.   In a way yes. The degree of negative liberty simply means how many doors are open to me, whether I want to go through them or not. If you call that "opportunity", that is in order, of course, but negative liberty by itself is not enough because there are other values, without pursuit of which life may not be worth living. I'm the last person to deny that. Liberty has to be restrained because of the claims—the basic needs—of security, happiness, justice, knowledge, order, social solidarity, peace. Certain forms of liberty must be restrained to make room for the other ultimate ends of life. As always, it is a matter of the kind of trade-offs which are required by a decent society.

R. J.   So, how can negative liberty work?

I. B.   It works because without it, there is suffocation. Negative liberty means the removal or absence of the obstacles which are not needed for the purpose of satisfying other ultimate human values. Without some restraint—*pace* Godwin, Kropotkin, Elisée Reclus—backed by the possibility of enforcement, neither social nor personal security, nor justice, nor happiness, nor knowledge can be enjoyed. But negative liberty is also such that in its absence other values collapse also, because there is no opportunity to practise them, there are no opportunities, no constellation of diverse values—in the end, no life.

OXFORD PHILOSOPHY AND POSITIVISM

R. J.   What is Oxford philosophy?

I. B.   It is a particular movement which began in the late 1930s and then expanded after the war and developed vigorously until the death of its real founder, a philosopher called John Austin, who died in 1959. Fundamentally Oxford philosophy was an examination of how various expressions were used to convey what, and how confusions were caused by mistaken identification of, or distinctions between words and expressions intended to be understood without any dogmatic rules about what was valid and what was not. The ultimate object of enquiry was the function of words, derived from that for which people used them in ordinary life—descriptive, exclamatory, performative, commands etc.—or in specialized disciplines—scientific, legal, religious, in works of fiction, and so on.

R. J.   Was it mainly against the Positivist current?

I. B.   No. It was a radical modification of it. But it was fundamentally against the view that scientific language was the model for other types of use of words, because, as some Positivists supposed, common sense language could always in principle be reduced to some degree of scientific exactness. "Oxford philosophy" was against that. It recognized the rich ambiguity of language, and difference of verbal uses, the inevitable ambivalence of words, and the dependence of inter-woven complexes of words on different angles of vision of reality. The example of the mirror I used before is quite a good early example of the approach of "Oxford philosophy". Logical Positivism was not the answer. As I told you before, the neglect of the ambiguity of the word "in" when we speak of an image *in* the mirror, can lead to avoidable philosophical confusions.

R. J.   Can one say that Oxford philosophy was mainly an empirical philosophy?

I. B.   Oh yes. It began with an examination of the ordinary sense in which words are used. This was regarded as a pointer to the kind of things which people observed or thought, and this cast doubts on the translation of the words into a more precise language which obeyed the rigid rules which the Positivists imposed upon the limits of meaning, in fact led to false accounts of what people wanted to say. In other words, it rested on the view that the meaning of the words depends on the way one used words, not on certain (semantic) rules governing the relation of words with things.

R. J.   I remember that in your essay on Austin, when you describe the atmosphere of Oxford philosophy, you speak of meetings and discussions. Did you take part in these discussions?

I. B.   I started them. The particular small group of which I wrote met in my rooms. It began in 1936 and went on until the war. There were very few of us. Austin and Ayer always came. After 1936 Stuart Hampshire was also present. Also Donald Macnabb who wrote a book on Hume and very occasionally Donald Mackinnon who became a professor of theology. We talked and argued. The trouble was that if we convinced each other, we thought that that was enough: no need to tell others, or to publish. All that mattered was that we—the little *cénacle*—had discovered something: the rest of the world was irrelevant. We had a sense of being original discoverers of important truths; it was very exhilarating, but self-centred: we saw no need to publish our results.

R. J.   How is it that you never accepted the issues of Positivism?

I. B.   I was not brought up as a Positivist. I was brought up originally as an English Hegelian. I rebelled against that, because I couldn't understand Hegelian language, and when I read the English Hegelians I found myself floating about in a kind of a mist which I really did not and still do not enjoy. I felt much the same when I read Bergson. I derived no light from such prose. So I became what is known as an Oxford Realist. That meant acceptance of the philosophical approach of thinkers like Bertrand Russell, G. E. Moore, Henry Price, Gilbert Ryle, William Kneale and four or five others. It all sprang initially from the writings of a forgotten Oxford philosopher at the turn of the century, aimed at refutation in dry Aristotelian terms of the prevailing Hegelian philosophy. Brentano was doing that kind of thing in Prague at about the same time. (He was the teacher of Tomas Masaryk.) So did various Americans and Scandinavians. It was a healthy deflationary process, which let the air out of many philosophical balloons, and conveyed a strong sense of reality. Above all it stressed clarity of thought and language, and was a great relief after the metaphysical rhetoric and mists of Idealism. Then came the Vienna Circle and their British disciple A. J. Ayer—Carnap's pupils in America and

England, interest in logic and scientific method. There was a new philosophical magazine in which these discussions took place, as well as contributions to established journals, meetings in London of the new *philosophes* which I attended, but I found that some of their doctrines didn't appear to me to be valid—for instance, the central view that the meaning of a proposition was the means of its verification—some statements—for example general propositions ("all S is P")—did not seem to me in principle verifiable; falsifiable, yes, but how can one verify unlimited universal statements? One cannot verify by observation or experiment propositions which refer to an infinite number of instances. The Positivist answer was: "Very well, you can't literally verify it, but if you take the general proposition that all S is P, in conjunction with a singular proposition, this could lead to another singular proposition." For example, take a general proposition: "All men are mortal" and a particular proposition: "Socrates is a man" then "Socrates is mortal" would follow, that might be verifiable by his death. But from this it seems to follow that general propositions were not descriptive, as they claimed to be. They are just instruments for deriving one singular proposition from another. I didn't believe that. I thought that when we say: "All S is P," we meant to say exactly that: that "All Ss are Ps,"—a factual statement, whether formal or empirical, however many Xs there were, whether a finite or an infinite number. Then I began getting puzzled about what were called "counter factual propositions"—unfulfilled hypotheticals. "If you had looked out of the window you would have seen a man." How does one verify that? I didn't look out of the window, so how could I tell what I would have seen. All I can say is: "Anybody who looked out would have seen a man" or "everyone who looked out of the window at a certain time could have seen this man". But "would" and "could" are not directly verifiable: the act might not have taken place. I thought and think that propositions have meaning whether or not one knew of any means of completely verifying them, imperfect verification did not mean that their meaning was somehow imperfect; the meaning of all kinds of singular propositions could not be solely their means of verification.

R. J.   And that is what you tried to expose in your three essays against Positivism?

I. B.   Yes.

R. J.   Were these your first essays?

I. B.   I think they were my first professional essays. I can't remember in what order they appeared. I think the first one was a paper on "Induction and Hypothesis" published in one of the volumes of the Aristotelian Society. The Aristotelian Society is a philosophical society, not particularly Aristotelian: it is simply called after Aristotle. It might just as well have been called Platonic or Cartesian or Lockean or Kantian. Its publications constitute the development of British philosophy, certainly in this century.

BERGSON, SCHELLING AND ROMANTICISM

R. J.   You talked previously about Bergson. Did he influence you?

I. B.   Not at all. I read *Évolution Créatrice*, but it made no impression on me, I'm sorry to say. But I did read two good books by Bergson, one is *Essai sur les Données Immédiates de la Conscience* which is a very intelligent piece of empirical descriptive psychology. If you say that one headache is more violent than another, you cannot say twice or five times as violent; "more" and "less" can be measured in one sphere, but not in another. There is a very definite distinction between "intensive" and "extensive" magnitude, those of extent and those of degree, expressible in cardinal and ordinal numbers which govern our language and ideas. The other book was *Les Deux Sources de la Morale et de la Religion*, which I think was perhaps his last book, where he compares the Kantian ethics which he is against—the ethics of rules and imperatives—to something like morality based on the imitation of the life of the saints. This book seems to me interesting—much better than his more famous and influential books—but I did not accept either its argument or its conclusions which seem to me purely subjective meditation, autobiographical, but neither rigorous, nor convincing.

R. J.   Do you feel close to what we call "vitalist philosophy"?

I. B.   Not particularly. I think there is some truth in what they say. I think vitalist philosophy is something which has to do with romanticism. I have studied romanticism quite closely. But I think that vitalism is founded on a metaphor. The metaphor is that all true thought and experience should be understood in terms of a biological organism. Well, sometimes this is illuminating, sometimes not. As you know romanticism historically came before the vitalist philosophy. In Leibniz there are certain elements of it, of course, and perhaps even in Aristotle, but romanticism rests on a view that there is no fixed order of Nature which science (or philosophy) can study, there is no *rerum natura*, there is a perpetual cosmic growth or process, a movement or self-realization by the Cosmos, Spirit or Nature, to which we belong and any attempt to arrest this for inspection and analysis kills it. Goethe once said of Moses Mendelssohn's aesthetic methods that he kills the butterfly, pins it down and the creature loses all colour, all that lives and moves; he dissects a corpse not something in living Nature. There is a lot of this in Bergson of course. Bergson was a super-romantic philosopher. He has little to do with classical philosophy. He was influenced by Ravaisson, and Ravaisson was influenced by Schelling. There is nothing in Bergson of Descartes or Malebranche or Locke or Kant or Renouvier.

R. J.   Bergson is a very anti-intellectualist philosopher.

I. B.   To an extent, yes. He thinks that intellectualism is analysis and the analysis arrests the flow. Vitalism of course says that things are explained in terms of the development of growth. But it seems to me that Bergson's ideas come from the teleological biology of the eighteenth century, which was given a tremendous lift philosophically by the romantic philosophers like Schelling, Fichte and to some degree Hegel, and the German philosophy of that time, and also by Maine de Biran.

R. J.   Who is your favourite thinker in the German Romantic current, Novalis, the Schlegel brothers?

I. B.   Novalis said a great many profound things. Some-times it's crazy, but sometimes it's wonderful. Friedrich Schlegel is often vague, cloudy and obscure, but there are marvellous insights. His brother August Schlegel is of less interest to me. He was a friend of Madame de Staël, I think a tutor to her children, and greatly expanded the limits of the history of literature. Schelling's writing contains inspired passages. Again, sometimes it's all darkness; but then he comes out of the wood into a kind of clearing, and then one can understand what he is saying about genius, about art, and that's absolutely wonderful. Schelling's *Aesthetics* is remark-ably illuminating.

R. J.   Schelling had a lot of influence on European thought in the nineteenth century.

I. B.   Yes, he had a great influence on the French. I don't know who translated Schelling into French, but he indirectly influenced French poets like Nerval, the young Théophile Gautier and, perhaps, even Victor Hugo, who knows? German metaphysics was fashionable via Mme de Staël and Edgar Quinet, and influenced minor romantics, like Petrus Borel[1]. Some among them were not greatly talented, but they were read, and they contributed to the general climate of ideas out of which romanticism grew.

R. J.   So, do you feel closer to German romanticism than to French romanticism?

I. B.   Interested, very, but not close. Romanticism was basically invented by the Germans, in my opinion, partly as a result of a long humiliation of Germans by the dominant French, as an anti-Enlightenment reaction, Goethe had an ambivalent attitude to the romantics; he admired Herder— but on the whole he despised them. For more than two millennia people had believed that every genuine question must have one true answer and one only. After the romantics had done their work it began to be believed that some answers were not to be discovered, but created; that moral and political values are not found but made. I do not wish to maintain that this is true, but it is what some German romantics believed. And nationalism is a product of this: there were—and are—men and women who think and act as they do because they believe in some ideal, a way of life, simply and solely because it is German—our own. We Germans lead this form of life, not because it is good or bad, right or wrong, but because it is ours, created by our traditions, our forebears—it is our stream of life and devel-

---

1. Baudelaire dedicated an essay, "Le Lycanthrope", to Petrus Borel (1809–59), whom he appreciated as much as Aloysius Betrand. André Breton also respected the black humour of the author of *Champavert, Contes Immoraux* (1833).

opment, and because it is ours, our own, we are ready to defend it with our lives. Herzen once asked, "Where is the song before it is sung?" Where is the walk before I took it and measured what it is? Nowhere. Nowhere before we sang it. Before we created it, it does not exist. So with values, ideals, ways of living—made, created, not discovered. The basic art of original creation as opposed to discovery and analysis—that's a romantic conception. This contradicts the philosophy—the *philosophia perennis*, of objective values, however discovered, which reigned from Plato until the modern Positivists, throughout Western history with no break. This great structure was not overthrown, but it was cracked, as it were, by the romantics. As for us, we inherit both these traditions, objective discovery and subjective creation, and oscillate between them, and try vainly to combine them, or ignore their incompatibility.

FIFTH CONVERSATION

❖

Personal Impressions

NINETEENTH-CENTURY RUSSIAN THOUGHT

RAMIN JAHANBEGLOO   Maybe we can talk now about the Russian thinkers and the influence German romanticism had on them.

ISAIAH BERLIN   It was not profound. They read them, but if you ask about the direct impact of the romantics, Pushkin of course loved Byron and was inspired by him. Lermontov was also deeply influenced by Byron, and by some of the German romantic poets. They both read Byron in French. Not many in Russia at that time read English freely. Of course a good many of them read German. Zhukovsky, who was Pushkin's teacher, read Goethe—his translation of the *Erlkönig* is wonderful—and, I think, Heine too. Russian intellectuals were disciples of Germans because some of them, even in the eighteenth century, went to German universities, particularly Göttingen. They continued to do so particularly after the French Revolution, since the Russian government thought that France was obviously an ideologically dangerous country, whereas Germany was a politically safe collection of conservative principalities.

R. J.   Can you name some of the Russian thinkers who went to German universities?

I. B.   Zhukovsky went to Dorpat, a German-language university in Russian Estonia—the poetical Lensky, in Pushkin's *Eugene Onegin*, is described as having "a Göttingen soul". Turgenev, Bakunin, Stankevich, went to the university of Berlin, and elsewhere in Germany—one or two Russians corresponded with Schelling—Turgenev, Bakunin and their friends listened to lectures by German scholars and thinkers. And of course some Germans taught in Russian universities. It was natural, for instance, for Pasternak to go to Marburg to study philosophy under the neo-Kantian Hermann Cohen. So did Lenin's first Commissar of Justice. Russian historians were deeply influenced by the great German historical school.

R. J.   Paris was also considered a cultural Mecca for Russian intellectuals.

I. B.   Yes, in the eighteenth century, but in the nineteenth century, Paris is the Mecca of left-wing political thinkers, because that is where you could find Saint-Simon, Fourier, Louis Blanc, Blanqui, Leroux, Proudhon, Marx and others. Russian exiles went to Paris because it was in a state of political ferment.

R. J.   How did Hegel and Hegelianism come to dominate the thought of young Russian intellectuals?

I. B.   First of all because Hegel was the dominant German philosopher, and Russia at that time was intellectually a province of Germany. Russian universities were fed intellectually from German streams in the first half of the nineteenth century.

R. J.   But was Hegel translated into Russian?

I. B.   Yes, of course. But they read him in German.

Bakunin read German, so did Herzen and Turgenev. Belinsky did not, Bakunin explained to him what Hegel taught. There were endless discussions in Moscow and Petersburg of German metaphysics, especially about the philosophy of history and ethics.

R. J.   But Bakunin was very anti-German.

I. B.   But not anti-Hegelian. He began as a left-wing Hegelian. He was anti-Prussian politically.

R. J.   He seems to be very anti-Prussian in his discussions with Marx.

I. B.   That is so. But, as you know, Bakunin was the first translator of *Das Kapital* into Russian, only of one volume—after which there was a quarrel, talk of blackmail, and goodness knows what.

R. J.   And Nechaev?

I. B.   All this is before Nechaev.

NECHAEV AND NIHILISM

R. J.   What do you think of Nechaev?

I. B.   Well, he is beautifully described by Dostoevsky in his novel *The Devils*. Nechaev was a little deranged, he had criminal tendencies, he deceived Bakunin and Ogarev in Switzerland, he was a violent terrorist and a mindless fanatic who did quite a lot of damage to the cause of Russian liberation. Of course he had the courage of a dedicated zealot. I remember that when conspirators came to see him in prison in 1881 and said that they had enough means either to help him to escape or assassinate the Tsar, but not for both attempts—which were they to do? "Kill the Tsar" he said without hesitation and died in prison. He seems to have had much personal charm. The warders in the Peter and Paul Fortress in which he was confined, were beguiled by him.

R. J.   Do you consider Nechaev the main figure of Russian nihilism?

I. B.   No. He is a marginal figure. Who were the nihilists? There was no party which called itself "nihilist". "Nihilism" is only a word used by their opponents who accused them of denying all moral values. There was in Russia a party of revolutionary terrorists, a kind of extreme Jacobins, a group in the 1860s called "Hell", *Ad* in Russian. There was a much larger populist group called "Land and Liberty" and various factions within these. Karakozov, who was a member of "Hell", made an attempt on Alexander II; the Tsar was later assassinated by a member of a conspiratorial group called "the People's Will" connected with "Land and Liberty"[1]. The Russian radical Left did not have an official name. For example, the group to which Dostoevsky belonged in the late eighteen forties—and for which he was condemned to death—were Fourierists—the so-called "Petrashevsky Circle". Herzen's and Bakunin's circles had no name, no organization, a somewhat general programme, no precisely formulated positive aims.

---

1. Karakozov's attempt to assassinate the Tsar took place in April 1866; he was finally assassinated on 1 March 1881. The extremist faction which he organized was led by Andrey Zheliabov and Sophie Perovskaya, the daughter of a general.

TURGENEV

R. J.   Can one draw a parallel between Nechaev and the figure of Bazarov in Turgenev's *Fathers and Children*?

I. B.   Not at all. Bazarov is not at all a Nechaevist—he had nothing to do with terror and he is a passionate believer in scientific truth and rational conduct based on it.

R. J.   But he is a nihilist.

I. B.   That's what he is called by one of the figures in the novel *Fathers and Children*. Turgenev virtually invented the term—at least he gave it circulation. Nobody knows who exactly first used the word "nihilist". It is thought to come from the French *rienisme* or a German author. All it came to mean is a rejection of everything which cannot be scientifically proved. It does not mean rejection of all values. It doesn't mean general rejection of absolutely everything that the bourgeoisie believes. Anything can be believed, provided it can be rationally established. The man who wrote most eloquently about that was Pisarev. He was, one could say, much more the original of Bazarov. Turgenev claimed to have admired Bazarov, but this was a defensive move against attacks from the Left. The men he knew best among these people were the critics Chernyshevsky and Dobrolyubov. Chernyshevsky is the true father of Russian populist Socialism, greatly admired by Lenin; he was thought dull, dreary and very inferior equally by Turgenev, Tolstoy, Herzen and Dostoevsky.

They all spoke of him as a tedious, third-rate, pedestrian figure who didn't understand life or literature or what men lived by. Dobrolyubov was a much livelier literary critic, a sharp radical who wrote a very critical review of Turgenev's novel *On the Eve*.

R. J.   How did you come to work on Turgenev?

I. B.   By reading him. Just like that.

R. J.   You translated Turgenev's *First Love*.

I. B.   I also translated two other things. A little story called *A Fire at Sea* which is a short piece and *A Month in the Country*, a play. It was performed recently at the National Theatre.

R. J.   Was it a commission?

I. B.   Yes. I was asked to do it by Peter Hall, the director. *First Love* was commissioned by the publisher Hamish Hamilton. *A Fire at Sea* was not commissioned. That was a story which fascinated me, because it was so totally autobiographical. So is *First Love*.

R. J.   But maybe you feel much closer to Turgenev's *Fathers and Children*?

I. B.   I suppose so. I based a lecture on it, later published. I consider *Fathers and Children* a political masterpiece.

R. J.   Turgenev seems to have suffered a lot, as you say in your essay on him.

I. B.   Yes. Tolstoy thought him shallow. The revolutionaries thought he was not left-wing enough. The reactionaries thought him a wicked radical. He never belonged to any party.

R. J.   How is it that he is still unknown as a Russian political thinker?

I. B.   He is a novelist and an essayist, not a political thinker. He is a typical gradualist liberal of Western type. His ideas were not very original, but he was a marvellous novelist, extremely sensitive, intelligent, ironical, realistic, very attractive as a man, but not terribly brave. He was no more a political thinker, say, than Sainte-Beuve or Victor Hugo.

R. J.   In your essay, you point out the fact that "by temperament Turgenev was not politically minded and he was often described as a pure aesthete and a believer in art for art's sake".

I. B.   That was true both during his life-time and after. But in fact most of his novels are deeply concerned with the conflicts in Russia. French writers thought him an exquisite writer. It was Flaubert, I think, who gave him the reputation of being an aesthete. Henry James agreed with this, and visited him and adored him. And he is an aesthete, a wonderful stylist. He is indeed the best Russian stylist since Pushkin. But, of course, no decent Russian in the nineteenth century could fail to be upset by the regime; and if you were a writer you felt a duty to say these things in public. Turgenev's novels are deeply concerned with social issues in Russia: he had a political position. So, too, Belinsky, who was a passionate moral and social thinker, was in theory nothing but a literary critic. He had a very considerable influence on Herzen and Turgenev, in some ways on Dostoevsky, but very little on Tolstoy.

R. J.   You make a parallel in your essay between Herder and Turgenev by claiming that "Turgenev possessed in a highly developed form what Herder called *Einfühlen* [empathy]."

I. B.   Yes, Turgenev had this empathetic insight, because he understood peasants, for example, in fact better than Tolstoy understood them. Tolstoy's peasants are idealized figures made of paper. Turgenev's peasants are absolutely genuine. Perhaps Tolstoy was a trifle jealous. Turgenev in a letter, says something like (I do not remember the exact text), "I had a curious dream. I dreamt that I was sitting on the verandah of my country house when suddenly a group of peasants from my estate appeared before me, and they said: 'Master, we have come to hang you; but there is no hurry, if you would like to say your prayers before we do it, please do so.'" That's very typical of Turgenev: the peasants are perfectly decent, good people, rather gentle and courteous, who want to hang the master because this seems right to them. Tolstoy would never have allowed that.

R. J.   How do you consider Bazarov? Do you consider him to be the first Bolshevik?

I. B.   Yes. He is an extremist, he rejects all bourgeois culture and literature, he thinks all that of no value. The only thing which is worth anything in his eyes, is scientific materialism, which tells us how to shape life in accordance with what science teaches about the Nature in which we live. He is a man of feeling, but he has persuaded himself to reject art, idealism, liberalism, toleration of other opinions. His social fanaticism is typical of the Bolshevik Party.

R. J.   Or of an anarchist.

I. B.   No. Anarchists are not intolerant. They are not against artists. They are against authority and the State, but they are, of course, not against imagination, beauty, literature, personal relations. Life, thought, emotions must be free.

R. J.   But what you said yesterday about Bakunin's will to

170

destroy the universities is a kind of intolerance and fanaticism. Isn't it?

I. B.   Certainly. But that is not typical anarchist doctrine. That's just Bakunin.

R. J.   So from your point of view, the figure of Bazarov is not closer to Bakunin or Nechaev?

I. B.   No. Much closer to the publicist Pisarev. Nechaev is very perverted. He is a liar and manipulator, totally unscrupulous. He told Bakunin that there was a powerful pro-Bakunin movement in Russia, when there was nothing of the kind, he told him how they were organized. Naturally Bakunin became over excited and acted accordingly—you can read it all in an excellent book in French called *La Violence dans la Violence* by Michel Confino, a distinguished Israeli historian of Russia.

R. J.   How is it that Turgenev came to be so fascinated by the figure of Bazarov?

I. B.   Turgenev wanted to understand the young. All his life he wanted to understand what young men felt, he wanted to be liked by them. He detested reactionaries and was fascinated by their opponents. He thought that some of them—the Bazarovs—the so-called "Men of the Sixties"—went too far and feared the consequences, but he wanted to be liked by them, to earn their sympathies. Bazarov for him represented the reaction against his own generation—the liberals of the 1840s. Turgenev was frightened by them, but at the same time fascinated.

DOSTOEVSKY

R. J.   Do you think one could make a parallel between the figure of Bazarov and one of the characters in Dostoevsky's *The Devils*?

I. B.   No, because Dostoevsky really did hate radicals. He was one himself, as you know, before 1849. Anyway, he began to think that these people were destructive materialists who worked against the salvation of man by Christian faith—a Satanic force. When he heard that Nechaev had been involved in killing a man in his own party, ostensibly a traitor, but actually because he thought that complicity in a crime would serve to knit the group more closely, he became convinced that that is what all revolutionaries come to. *The Devils* is a reference to the *New Testament*—Christ causes diabolical possession to enter the Gadarene swine, and they drown themselves. That is the text from which Dostoevsky took the concept of "devils". He thought that revolutionaries can infect ordinary people with this Satanic madness until they too inevitably destroy themselves. Revolution for Dostoevsky was a path to self-destruction, and Nechaev was an extreme example of what a revolutionary mentality could lead to: lies, moral perversion, murder, the sin against the Holy Ghost, total dehumanization.

R. J.   Don't you think Dostoevsky is a kind of a prophet, when he predicts in his own way the coming of the Russian Revolution and Stalinism?

I. B.   Yes. I am sure he would have reacted in the same way as Solzhenitsyn does today. Solzhenitsyn thinks he is like Tolstoy, but he is much more like Dostoevsky.

R. J.   Why did Dostoevsky denounce Turgenev?

I. B.   Because he thought he was a Westerner and consequently a traitor to the aspirations of the Russian spirit. He told him that in Baden-Baden. Turgenev was a liberal, a member of the intelligentsia, whereas salvation was in Holy Russia, and her alone.

R. J.   How is it that you never wrote on Dostoevsky?

I. B.   I realize that he is a great genius, but I don't find his philosophy of life very sympathetic, it's too religious for me, and too clerical. Besides, when I read Dostoevsky I become unnerved—he can completely dominate one. One suddenly finds oneself in a nightmare, one's world becomes obsessive, turns into something sinister, one wants to escape from it. I don't want to write about that. It's too strong, too dark, too terrifying, for me. I am hopelessly secular. It is the kind of Christianity where saintliness borders on madness.

R. J.   Like Kafka?

I. B.   No, Kafka is more sympathetic. He is more realistic. In Kafka everything is described with a certain irony and the objects are quite natural. Dostoevsky is like a magnifying glass. If you hold a magnifying glass over a piece of paper in the light, it scorches it. The paper becomes distorted. That's what Dostoevsky does to reality. The light is so strong that it burns it. That was said by the critic Mikhailovsky, and it is true. He called Dostoevsky "a cruel talent". He is at times too savage, like D. H. Lawrence or Knut Hamsun.

R. J.   Well, that's the light of genius.

I. B.   No, the fire. Reality becomes distorted.

R. J.   Do you agree with Sergey Bulgakov, when he claims that Dostoevsky expressed through his novels the moral pain and the sickness of the conscience of the Russian intelligentsia?

I. B.   No, I do not. Because I'm on the side of the Russian intelligentsia—essentially sane, if troubled, people—and against Bulgakov. Bulgakov was one himself once, but he was converted. He made that remark after he became a priest. After the Revolution of 1905 those who looked for spiritual salvation thought that the Russian intelligentsia had gone wrong. 1905 was a kind of bankruptcy for them. They began on the Left, and they turned sharply to the Right, against radical reform, against all political action—and turned inwards, and sought salvation in individual self-transformation.

R. J.   Did Berdyaev change in the same way?

I. B.   Yes.

R. J.   How about Shestov?

I. B.   I admire him greatly. Berdyaev is an extremely intelligent man, and when he writes about the origins of Communism, or the ideas of Russian thinkers he can be extremely shrewd, but his own theological writings are not the kind of things which I understand. I am just not theologically minded. Shestov, I think, is a marvellous writer, a free spirit. He is an original thinker, not bound by philosophical dogma. He is sensitive, tolerant, with deep philosophical understanding. Above all, he does not exaggerate.

R. J.   But did you know him?

I. B.   No. I didn't know he existed. I discovered him after his death. His real name was Schwarzman. He was a Russian Jew. He never converted, even though he came close to some of the teachings of the Orthodox Church, because, we are told, he thought this might give too much pain to his father. Do people read Shestov in France?

R. J.   Well, he is not a very well-known author. Maybe because his books were translated many years ago and you can't find them easily in the bookshops.

I. B.   A pity. He has been translated into English, but the translation is not very recent either. When I give Shestov's books to anybody, they are usually delighted. There are two authors whom I make propaganda for: one is Herzen, the other is Shestov. They are both totally decent, open-minded, open-hearted human beings, as Dostoevsky was not.

ALEXANDER HERZEN

R. J.   Speaking of Herzen, why do you think that Herzen still remains an unknown thinker?

I. B.   Because he was not translated. Herzen's auto-biography was fully translated into French only about six years ago. It was translated into English before the war, but few people knew it; now it has been published in four excellently produced volumes, to which I wrote the introduction. I think he is now more widely read, but not very widely, not like Chekhov or Turgenev. The English take their time to welcome foreign writers.

R. J.   What influence did Herzen have on Russian political thought?

I. B.   There is disagreement about that. A book has just been published in America on this, which I haven't read. To begin with, Herzen is one of the fathers of Russian radicalism, and agrarian Socialism. He was the best known of the Russian émigrés and started the first revolutionary publication after he settled in London, directed against the Tsarist regime; he knew famous Western liberals like Michelet, Hugo, Mazzini, Garibaldi and they respected him. So the idea that Russia was not a motionless despotism, that there was movement inside it in favour of a freer society, became known to the West. Michelet was anti-Russian, and a Polonophile. There is a famous letter from Herzen to Michelet, to refute the idea that Russia was simply a huge, barbarian mass. Herzen is important because he is the true father of Russian radicalism, of social protest, brilliantly conducted. The earliest Socialist group in Russia is probably that to which the young Dostoevsky belonged. The view that this circle—the Fourierist group of the Petrashevtsy— was just a handful of unorganized dissident students is not true: they formulated and conspired to realize a full Socialist programme; this had a great deal of influence. Chernyshevsky, for example, was influenced by it, so was the famous satirist Saltykov. But Herzen was far more gifted than the others, and so he is—as Lenin conceded—the founder of Russian anti-monarchist public agitation. By the 1860s, the Russian Leftists thought that he was too moderate, too liberal, not ferocious enough, but still it was he who got them going. He was the first man to celebrate the Decembrists as fighters for freedom, and he was a friend and ally of Italian and French revolutionaries. Proudhon, Louis Blanc, Ledru-Rollin, Mazzini and others. He was the voice of Russia for them. His periodicals published in London, the *Polar Star*, *The Bell* and so on, were the *samizdat* of the time and fed, with other forbidden writings, the revolutionary movement in Russia. He became an icon, worshipped in the Soviet Union, although, paradoxically, he was violently opposed to Communism and particularly disliked and despised Marxism and Marxists. Indeed, Marx refused to go to a banquet in favour of oppressed Poland because Herzen would be present—Marx had considerable contempt for Slavs until right at the end of his life, when he slightly relented.

R. J.   Do you still believe that Herzen belonged to this type of men who live near the frontier that divides old from new?

I. B.   Yes. Herzen said of his circle in Moscow: "We were a kind of Janus." He met and was on terms with Slavophiles in the salons in Moscow, and wrote that while some of us looked to the West and others looked to the Slav past, one heart beat in us all.

R. J.   As you point out in your essay, Herzen was anxious to do something memorable for himself and for his country.

I. B.   He was certainly ambitious, and Belinsky encouraged him. Belinsky was at that time a famous radical critic who died in 1848, and after he read Herzen's novel *Who is to Blame?* he told him that he would survive not only in the history of Russian literature, but in Russian history. That turned out to be true. Herzen's novels are not first-rate, but they were very significant and politically deeply informative.

R. J.   How do you consider Herzen's *My Past and Thoughts*?

I. B.   *My Past and Thoughts* is a work of genius. It consists of the most marvellous memoirs of the entire nineteenth century, certainly the best since Rousseau, and I think in some ways even better than Rousseau. It is an incomparable masterpiece.

R. J.   Herzen seems also to be influenced by Hegel.

I. B.   Everybody in Moscow and Petersburg universities was influenced by Hegel at that time. I don think these Russians realized how conservative Hegel was, except Belinsky, who did, although Russian Marxists have never admitted this. They regard Belinsky as a great man, so if he seems to oppose Hegel, he must have misunderstood him. In fact, he understood him only too well. He read Hegel in Russian or French; Belinsky knew no German.

R. J.   Why do you think Herzen wrote *My Past and Thoughts*? I ask you this question, because I think that *My Past and Thoughts* is committed to no thesis.

I. B.   He wrote it, partly in order to try to get his terrible unhappiness out of his system. His adored wife ran away with a German poet called Georg Herwegh, a friend of Marx and Wagner; Herzen came to look on him as a shameless seducer, and was terribly upset. His wife did return to him and soon afterwards died. His mother and one of his small children were shipwrecked on the way to Nice, where he was waiting for them. So 1850–1 were very dark years for him. Partly to relieve his feelings he began writing a journal, and that continued for years. To write things down sometimes makes them more bearable. He was a marvellously gifted writer—and a personality of the first order. Even so highly critical and malicious a social observer as Edmond de Goncourt was impressed by him when they met in a salon in Paris in later years. He was a man of enormous vitality, and exceptional charm and courage.

R. J.   And you believe that Herzen is at the origins of the strong tradition of libertarian humanism in Russian Socialism which was defeated in 1917?

I. B.   Yes. Although as I told you, he is an official Communist saint.

R. J.   So he continued to be read by the Russians after 1917?

I. B.   Oh yes. Before 1905 he was censored in Russia. Herzen published pamphlets partly in German, partly in French. The first Russian edition of his memoirs appeared in 1905 during the first Russian Revolution, after that I don't think it was suppressed again.

R. J.   In your essay on Herzen you make a parallel between him and Bakunin by saying that both placed the idea of individual liberty at the centre of their thought. But I think there were great differences between the two men?

I. B.   Yes, of course, and Herzen knew that. But Herzen liked Bakunin personally. He didn't know that Bakunin had written a famous "Confession", I mean, a letter to the Tsar written in prison denying and disowning everything—a really grovelling document (which in fact did him no good)—it was only published in 1923. But in demanding individual liberty Bakunin went much farther. Herzen did not believe in *putsches*, a real revolution could only succeed after a process of education and preparation. A premature *putsch* would guarantee that all the vices of the old regime would re-emerge in some form in the new one. He once wrote that—I again, as so often, quote from memory—that one can't build a house for free people out of the bricks of a prison house. In an open letter to Bakunin, Herzen tells him that the methods of Attila, "Petrograndism", as he called it, will not work. He meant by that, that to create a revolution before the people are ready, and before they know how to live in freedom, means that they will retain the old habits of the prisoners, and there will be no gain.

R. J.   So is that the reason why you think that Herzen is very close to John Stuart Mill or Tocqueville?

I. B.   Only to some extent—not entirely. He didn't like Tocqueville who had behaved disagreeably to him. In 1848, Herzen went to a political meeting in Paris and was duly arrested by the police. He was being taken to the police station when he met Tocqueville on the way. Tocqueville was Minister of Foreign Affairs of the Second Republic at that time. He asked Tocqueville whom he had met before to identify and liberate him. He writes that Tocqueville replied that he was afraid that there was no connection between the judiciary and the executive. These were quite different powers, so he could do nothing. Naturally Herzen did not think well of this reaction. Tocqueville was a cold-hearted man, and didn't want to get mixed up with an obscure Russian agitator.

R. J.   That's quite amazing because Tocqueville is a severe critic of bureaucratic power.

I. B.   Tocqueville was very cautious. I wonder whether Tocqueville would have joined the French Resistance during the war. He would not have collaborated with the Nazis perhaps, but I don't think he would have joined the underground. Herzen would have done so.

R. J.   Herzen is a more romantic thinker than Tocqueville.

I. B.   He was just braver. He had always fought for his convictions.

R. J.   Why do you think Herzen turned to the West, instead of being a Slavophile?

I. B.   Because he thought the Slavophiles were wrong. The West did not employ serfs, the West was on the way to democracy, Western life was obviously much freer, personal dignity was respected in the West, as it was not in Russia.

Decent Russians with a sense of human dignity, and a desire to help the oppressed, turned to the West; even the Slavophiles were against Russian bureaucracy and the state control of Nicholas I: they were in favour of a kind of free theocracy which they imagined had reigned before Peter the Great, perhaps before Ivan the Terrible—a kind of Utopia. Herzen turned to the West, mainly because in Russia there was barbarism, slavery, oppression, ignorance, censorship and the whip. Innocent people were, at the whim of landowners or officials, beaten violently or sent to Siberia. In the West, by and large, they were not.

R. J.   What was the impact of the controversy between the Westerners and Slavophiles in Russian literature?

I. B.   The principal Slavophile poet is Apollon Grigoriev. The great Gogol, too, was close to the Slavophiles. He was not one, but he was well thought of by some of them, because he was pious and right-wing. Dostoevsky and Leskov were fellow travellers of Slavophiles of a peculiar kind. There was a great Slavophile poet, Tyutchev, perhaps the greatest Russian poet after Pushkin. He was a diplomat by profession, he had served in Westphalia and in Turin—a marvellous metaphysical poet. He had strong Slavophile sympathies, although he is not usually classified with them.

R. J.   So what was the impact of Western ideas in Russia in the 1840s?

I. B.   Well, philosophically very strong. French and German philosophers made a great impact on Russian academic and intellectual life. Kant, Fichte, Hegel, Schelling, Saint-Simon, Fourier, were widely known. In the 1820s the Russian universities taught German metaphysics; then the universities were shut down, in part because these—indeed all—philosophers were regarded as subversive by the Church and by the government. But philosophy was still taught in disguise. There was a philosopher called Pavlov who pretended that he was a biologist and he began his lectures by saying: "You wish to know Nature. But what is knowledge? What is Nature?" and after that expounded Schelling.

R. J. What were the origins of the Russian intellectual movement?

I. B. You could say that it began in the late eighteenth century more or less in the reign of Catherine the Great, when Diderot, Voltaire, Maupertuis, were in fashion. There was a small group of minor Russian *lumières* who tried to reform the education of well-born young men and, now and then, of the sons of priests and the like. The real intelligentsia is born sometime in the nineteenth century after the Napoleonic invasion when Russian officers marched victoriously into Paris, and were deeply impressed by what—in comparison with their own—seemed to them a liberal and enlightened society. That is when foreign ideas began to enter Russia in increasing volume, at first in aristocratic circles—Pushkin and his friends—a little later among humbler folk. Efforts were made by the authorities to curtail or stop the circulation of these—indeed all—ideas, but the process continued, Western doctrines were systematically smuggled into Petersburg and Moscow and caused considerable intellectual (and moral and political) ferment from then on.

INTELLECTUALS AND THE INTELLIGENTSIA

R. J. As you say, the word "intelligentsia" is a Russian word, but was it invented at that time?

I. B.   It is a Russian word. Some Poles think they invented the word "intelligentsia", but it is a Russian word. The word was invented only in the 1870s. Nobody spoke about "intelligentsia", under that title until then. So the word was invented much later to describe a phenomenon which by then had existed for half a century[2].

R. J.   What is the difference between the concept of "intelligentsia" and the concept of "intellectual"?

I. B.   Intellectuals are people who are simply interested in ideas, they want ideas to be as interesting as possible, as aesthetes are people who want things to be as beautiful as possible. The intelligentsia, historically, are people who are united around certain social ideas, who believe in progress, in reason, reject traditionalism, believe in scientific methods, free criticism, individual liberty, in short oppose reaction, obscurantism, the Church and the authoritarian state, and see each other as fellow fighters in a common cause—above all for human rights and a decent social order. One of them, writing in the 1860s, described them as resembling an Order of Knights bound by an oath, champions of an endangered ideal. You could say that the *philosophes* in eighteenth-century Paris were an intelligentsia because Diderot, D'Alembert, Holbach, Helvétius and Condorcet felt a sense of intellectual and moral brotherhood: they knew each other, they discussed the same ideas, they shared a common position, they were persecuted by the same people, the enemies were the Church, the absolute state—the *infâme* which tried to suppress truth and freedom—they felt themselves to be fighters for the light. The intelligentsia is founded on faith in enlightenment, which must be promoted against its enemies. That is why the intelligentsia—as

2. "The Birth of the Russian Intelligentsia" (1955), reprinted in *Russian Thinkers*.

a conscious formation—is more liable to happen where there exists a powerful and reactionary Church, for example, Roman Catholicism or the Orthodox Church. Hence the intelligentsia in France, in Italy, in Spain, in Russia. There is no real intelligentsia in Scandinavia or England. The Protestant churches are not felt to be a serious menace to liberal and progressive ideas.

R. J.   But you have intellectuals?

I. B.   Yes, certainly, and radicals too, and so on. This is not the same. There is no sense of solidarity—of being embattled between them, because the Church of England is not something which writers or scholars, or educated people in general, feel a need to fight against. It's not a great oppressive, powerful organization which dominates the social and the political scene. The Russian church was a firm ally of the Russian Tsarist system, and the intelligentsia loathed it. That's why Dostoevsky is not a member of the intelligentsia, nor too, for that matter, Chekhov, nor Pushkin nor Tolstoy. Turgenev certainly is.

R. J.   They are intellectuals.

I. B.   Not always. I don't think you could say that Dostoevsky was an intellectual: indeed he hated them. Tolstoy thought nothing of them, Pushkin, Lermontov, Tyutchev, Chekhov, cannot possibly be called intellectuals any more than Dickens or Balzac; Flaubert, George Sand, Renan, Nietzsche, were. The Slavophiles are anything but intellectuals. They were theologically oriented writers. The idea of a religious intelligentsia meant nothing in the nineteenth century. In the twentieth century it began to have a meaning, because some theologians and clergymen developed left-wing tendencies like Berdyaev, Bulgakov, and clergymen up and down the country: "left-wing parsons" became a familiar description.

R. J.   Whom do you consider "intelligentsia" in today's world?

I. B.   I think there is something like a real intelligentsia in New York, partly Jewish. There is a sort of kinship among certain writers, critics, musicians, artists who wish to resist the Black Hundreds[3] as they were called in Tsarist Russia—the forces of philistinism and reaction. The Bloomsbury group were something like it, but not quite. There is none in Britain, maybe Mrs Thatcher will create one. I don't think we can speak of a "Soviet intelligentsia" because they were not a real intelligentsia. They were just literate people of no particular moral or political colour. But a real intelligentsia has survived in Russia and the other republics against all odds. This is a most wonderful thing. They are true heirs of the old civilized, humane intelligentsia. I don't know how they survived or were reborn—Glasnost revealed and liberated them. Sakharov was a typical member of the intelligentsia. I greatly lament his death—his voice was the voice of Herzen and his friends—miraculously preserved through all those terrible years.

R. J.   How about Solzhenitsyn?

I. B.   No. Solzhenitsyn is not: he is the voice of Dostoevsky.

R. J.   So the controversy between the Slavophiles and the Westerners continues in the Soviet Union?

3. "The Black Hundreds", term derived from the "*sotnia*" (Cossack military group), was a name given, by its opponents, to a violently reactionary and anti-Semitic populist movement in the last decades of the Tsarist regime.

I. B.   Yes, in a sense it does. Herzen's great liberal voice is heard again. The controversy continues, because as long as there is a command economy—plus a nationalist criterion of "un-Russian" activities, it will continue, and the party of freedom will react against it. Solzhenitsyn is not against authority. He is against a particular Communist authority. But Sakharov and his friends were against all forms of anti-democracy. Solzhenitsyn is not a democrat, nor is he a Slavophile. What does he care about Czechs or Poles or Slovenes? But, of course, one can oppose a wicked regime from many angles.

R. J.   But do you consider Solzhenitsyn an intellectual?

I. B.   Scarcely. He seems to me to be neither an intellectual, nor a Slavophile. Solzhenitsyn does not take the slightest interest in non-Russian Slavs. He is a Russian patriot and much more like one of the Old Believers in the seventeenth century who rose against Peter the Great and all the modernization which he introduced, and looked on the church reformed by the Patriarch Nikon as the work of Satan and Peter as a devil on the throne. They remained loyal to the old tradition, and refused to have any truck with the sinful reorganized Russian Empire. He seems to me someone similar to the Christians of that persuasion.

R. J.   But what role do you think modernization played in the making of the Russian intelligentsia?

I. B.   Well, of course one thing would not have happened without the other. Without modernization few Western ideas would have penetrated Russia. Peter the Great's capture of Riga and the Baltic Coast was described as hacking a window to the West.

R. J.   Do you feel close to the thought of what we call *Mittel Europa*?

I. B.   I don't feel *Mittel Europa* to be a distinct culture. It is just the successor of the old Austro–Hungarian Empire, and produced, and still produces, very good writers. It belongs to the body of Western civilization.

1848

R. J.   Let us go back to Russia. Why do you consider the year 1848 to be a landmark in Russian history[4]?

I. B.   Partly because of the famous conspiracy which Dostoevsky was part of, and partly because no revolution occurred in the Russian empire. Russian troops crushed the revolution in Budapest, Poland was crushed some years before, the pillars of the old regimes remained upright. Some Russian thinkers after 1848 thought that given the ease with which the left-wing revolutions collapsed in Paris and Germany, Western methods were perhaps not the way to freedom in Russia or anywhere else: the Western bourgeois liberals were not to be imitated. Both Chernyshevsky and Herzen, impressed by the failure of these revolutions, wondered whether there was a special Russian pathway to Socialism—what the Germans called *ein Sönderweg*. Herzen believed in development "through the peasant commune to Socialism", not through Socialism to the peasant commune. Russia must develop in its own way. In the West the revolutions of 1848 failed. The last thing Russia needs is industrial capitalism with a huge oppressed proletariat. One can build a freer and juster state without going through the

4.   "Russia and 1848" (1948), reprinted in *Russian Thinkers*.

horrors of Western industrialism. That's why 1848 is an important date for the Russian radicals. Herzen was deeply disappointed by what happened in Europe. But he had already attacked the French bourgeoisie earlier—in 1847. It was not the revolution of 1848 that turned him back towards Russia. He never turned away from it. He distrusted the French bourgeoisie before the revolution. If you read his *Letters from Avenue Marigny*, you'll find many biting things about it. He wrote that Figaro had the uniform of a lackey, but he was a free man when he took it off, but with these people, Figaro's uniform is part of their skin, they can't take it off, they are lackeys by nature. All this before 1848.

THE HEDGEHOG AND THE FOX

R. J.   I think one can say that in your classification of hedgehogs and foxes[5] you consider Herzen a fox.

I. B.   Absolutely.

R. J.   By the way, why did you make this classification?

I. B.   I never meant it very seriously. I meant it as a kind of enjoyable intellectual game, but it was taken seriously. Every classification throws light on something, this one was very simple.

R. J.   So you don't justify your classification?

I. B.   What do you mean by justification? Hedgehogs and

5. "The Hedgehog and the Fox" is an essay published in 1953, reprinted in *Russian Thinkers*. Isaiah Berlin quoted from a verse by the Greek poet Archilochus (7th century BC) which inspired his zoomorphic comparisons.

foxes? It is not exhaustive. Some people are neither foxes nor hedgehogs, some people are both.

R. J.   Let us take Pushkin for example, why do you consider him an arch-fox?

I. B.   Pushkin is not a man who tries to interpret everything in the light of some single all-embracing system. That's what hedgehogs do. He simply reacts as he reacts, he describes what he describes, writes what he writes. I mean, he expresses himself in many directions, as the spirit takes him. Whereas hedgehogs are always trying to connect, always trying to represent things as in some sense fitting or not fitting into some single pattern in which they passionately believe. They are constantly viewing things and measuring their significance in terms of some unifying principle, as opposed to being interested by things for their own sake.

R. J.   And do you really believe that Russian literature has two poles: Dostoevsky on the one hand, Pushkin on the other?

I. B.   There is Tolstoy too. Tolstoy is a fox who believed passionately in being a hedgehog. Dostoevsky is a real hedgehog. It is not a peculiarly Russian division. Goethe was a fox, and Hegel a hedgehog.

R. J.   Whom do you consider to be the two extremes of Russian literature?

I. B.   Well, Dostoevsky on one hand, Turgenev on the other. One can do it with any literature. In French literature you have Victor Hugo and Flaubert; Anatole France and Huysmans.

R. J.   In your essay, "The Hedgehog and the Fox", you

show how Tolstoy is in constant contradiction with himself, on the one hand in his artistic vision, and on the other hand in his vision of history.

I. B.   Yes, Tolstoy longed for a unitary vision, but his marvellous perception of people, things, situations, the moments of history, details for their own sake was so acute and irresistible that he couldn't refrain from simply writing as he saw, perceived, felt, thought, understood. But later he condemned all that because it didn't contribute to the vision which he developed later in life. That is what I mean.

R. J.   So, from your point of view, Tolstoy could be at the same time a monist and a pluralist thinker?

I. B.   He was pluralist by nature, but he believed in monism. He was a fox, who wanted to be a hedgehog. Hence the tension, particularly in his later oeuvre.

R. J.   You also make a parallel between Tolstoy and Maistre.

I. B.   Only because when they both describe wars and battles, they have a similar view of what happens and what causes it. Tolstoy read Maistre when he was preparing his account of the battle of Borodino; Maistre was in Petersburg at the time, and does describe some of what went on in the capital. He is a primary authority for certain Russian phenomena observed by a very intelligent foreigner. I don't think Tolstoy consciously imitated him, but Maistre's description of battles, his view that although generals think they command, and give orders, what happens bears no resemblance to their careful dispositions and depends on a mass of factors which neither they nor anyone can control; that victories and defeats depend on psychological factors to which the commanders are irrelevant—that is echoed by

Tolstoy with his contempt for Napoleon's vanity—the elaborate plans of German military experts, as against the intuitive sense of reality, and above all of what goes on in the minds and hearts of the soldiers, which he attributed to Kutuzov.

R. J.   But there is a kind of similarity between these two thinkers, when they both reject, as you claim, the concept of individual political liberty and when they are both sceptical about techniques?

I. B.   They are both anti-modern. Except that Maistre is in favour of authority, above all of the church, while Tolstoy thought it irrational and obviously oppressive, and rebelled against a state he regarded as at once stupid and immoral.

R. J.   Do you think one can also make a parallel between Tolstoy and Dostoevsky by taking into consideration the affinity which exists between the figure of Prince Muishkin in the *Idiot* and the figure of Pierre in *War and Peace*?

I. B.   They are both Christian figures, but there is a difference. Pierre is Tolstoy, after all. Pierre is a secular figure, whose instincts and feelings towards people and nature are absolutely natural and authentic. Muishkin is simply a sort of saint, an innocent victim, a saviour of souls, and a holy fool, not of this world—the world of triviality, materialists and sinfulness. One of my friends, a Russian thinker, once said, "The nearest person to Prince Muishkin in the twentieth century is Charlie Chaplin." I don't agree, but I know what he meant. Muishkin looks foolish, but fundamentally he represents the truth. Chaplin is a good man, in an immoral society—in his films he stands for decent, human feeling and kindness, *naiveté*, simplicity, childishness. Pierre is not childlike. He is naive in some ways but he is not childlike. After all Muishkin does go mad at the end, and goes back to

Switzerland, but Pierre marries Natasha and lives a normal life at the end of *War and Peace*. Pierre in early versions of the novel becomes a Decembrist—Dostoevsky is not interested in this at all. Muishkin is not interested in politics or social structures, he is like a saintly child who has an intuitive vision of the truth, Christ lives in him. He is one of the avatars of the Christ in literature.

BELINSKY

R. J.   Let us go back to the figure of Bazarov in Turgenev's *Fathers and Children*. How is it that you compare Belinsky to Bazarov?

I. B.   Because Belinsky was liable to say harsh things. He was a man who denounced what he regarded as feeble, bourgeois platitudes and salon art, aestheticism, hypocrisy, the detachment of art—especially flight from social reality; he was pro-Jacobin and he hated *le juste milieu*; that is why he disliked what seemed to him the smartness, superficiality, self-indulgence which he saw in Paris. He was a puritan and wanted clear distinctions, yes or no, black or white, with us or against us. That is how he resembles Bazarov. Belinsky is not a liberal, like Turgenev, nor a delightful personality like Herzen. He moved from doctrine to doctrine, his search for the truth—above all moral truth—was agonizing for him. His friends adored and pitied him. And respected him more than they did each other[6].

R. J.   But he is a Westerner.

6. Vissarion Belinsky (1811–48), the most famous nineteenth-century Russian critic, inspiring two generations of thought, especially the so-called Westernizers. He contributed to the liberal journal *Notes on the Fatherland* edited by Kraevsky (1840–41), and later to *The Contemporary* edited by the famous poet Nekrasov (1846–8). Berlin wrote on Belinsky in *Encounter*, 1955 (reprinted in *Russian Thinkers*).

I. B.   Yes, he is. Not by temperament, but by conviction. He did not enjoy his visits to the West. He did not like Dresden, he disliked Raphael's Sistine Madonna, nor did he enjoy being in Paris.

R. J.   Can you make a comparison between him and Herzen?

I. B.   They were genuine friends. Herzen is much more subtle. He is much more perceptive, he is much cleverer and more sensitive to the contours of Western civilization, to relations and absence of relations between Russia and the West. Belinsky is much simpler, more categorical, more black and white, more harsh, and deeply sincere, undeviatingly, unshirkingly honest and Herzen looked at him as a sort of conscience which kept them all on the right path. When Belinsky thought something was evil, he said so. No compromise. No escape from social problems into art's sake.

R. J.   What was Belinsky's intellectual position in nineteenth-century Russia?

I. B.   He died in early 1848 before all the European revolutions. He was acutely oppositional. He preached individual liberty, freedom of thought, he denounced the censorship, from which he suffered. He wanted a bill of human rights, respect for law, an end of arbitrary autocracy, serfdom, police and landowners' brutality. If you want to know what his final position was, the best statement of it is a famous piece called "Letter to Gogol", where he denounced Gogol's neo-feudalism. This document became the Bible of the Russian libertarian social and liberal movement through the nineteenth century, its noblest manifesto. In effect he said to Gogol: "How can you, a great artist, defend this abominable system?" It was a great call for decency, freedom, dedication to justice and truth.

R. J.   And Gogol published a pamphlet against him too.

I. B.   He did indeed. He wrote something called "Correspondence with Friends". But that was not widely read. Gogol was a real reactionary. He believed in family, church, landownership, serfdom. He knew what the serfs suffered, but didn't want to liberate them.

R. J.   What is Belinsky's conception of art?

I. B.   His conception of art was, in a way, rather crude. He was liable to go too far. Belinsky believed that the purpose of art was moral and social truth. He was an anti-aesthetic, against the ideal of pure art. His comments on literature are sometimes absurd. But his essays on Pushkin are a masterpiece. You must remember that in Belinsky's time, in that particular society, imaginative literature and art were the only regions—disguises—in which you could get round the censorship, and express political and social criticism. And he did this too, passionately, eloquently and movingly. Tolstoy began to think better of Belinsky towards the end of his life. But in the 1840s, 50s and 60s he thought Belinsky was a crude, inartistic hack, blind to what men lived by.

R. J.   He rejected the utilitarian doctrines of art?

I. B.   Yes, Chernyshevsky interpreted Belinsky in a utilitarian way, but that is wrong, Belinsky was not utilitarian. He believed that the purpose of art is to tell the truth as one saw it, by means of images, not propaganda. The truth is always social truth for him, because men live in society. All individuals live in a communal texture, hence true art, he believed, is necessarily social. He is no doubt mistaken: he is too puritanical, there is such a thing as pure art, but he did not like it, and saw it as mere escapism.

FROM PASTERNAK TO BRODSKY

R. J. Speaking of art, I would like to ask you a few questions in relation to Pasternak and Akhmatova. An hour ago, we were talking about Dostoevsky and Tolstoy and it's quite interesting to point out the fact as you do in your essay "Meetings with Russian Writers" that Akhmatova disliked Tolstoy and worshipped Dostoevsky.

I. B. That is so. It's quite difficult to talk about Akhmatova's view of life in a few sentences. She had a tragic view of life rather like Unamuno in Spain.

R. J. You have read Unamuno?

I. B. Yes.

R. J. Did you like him?

I. B. Very much. *The Tragic Sentiment of Life* is a very good book. Once I heard him lecture in Oxford, and found him deeply impressive. As for Akhmatova she said to me: "Tolstoy's morality is wrong. He shouldn't have condemned Anna Karenina. He knew better. That is the morality of his Moscow aunts. Monstrous!" Akhmatova didn't like Chekhov, because in him everything is low-toned, grey, the colour of mud—"no swords flash". The excellent critic D. S. Mirsky felt that too—so did others, but of course it is not a general view, rightly. Akhmatova believed in a life of passion, and profound religious and emotional tragic experience, which she did not find in Tolstoy. She found it in Dostoevsky and Kafka and Pushkin.

R. J. Was Pasternak very much influenced by Tolstoy?

I. B. Not all that much, but of course he knew Tolstoy

because his father did; and admired him immensely. He never talked to me about Russian literature, only about Shakespeare and Proust.

R. J. But as you say in your essay, Pasternak found it impossible to be critical towards Tolstoy because he thought Tolstoy and Russia were one.

I. B. That is true. He said that.

R. J. I didn't know that Pasternak had translated Shakespeare.

I. B. He translated *Hamlet*, and I believe other plays too.

R. J. Did he know English very well?

I. B. No, but he managed.

R. J. Can you say a few words about your meeting with Sergey Eisenstein?

I. B. Well, I've said all that in my essay in *Personal Impressions*. I have nothing to add. He was a charming, greatly gifted man. I liked him very much.

R. J. How about Joseph Brodsky? You say that he was very close to Akhmatova.

I. B. He was. She told me that she more or less brought him up by hand. He admired and adored her. Mandelshtam, Akhmatova and Tsvetaeva he loves greatly, much more than Pasternak and Blok. Mandelshtam, Akhmatova and Tsvetaeva, yes, and Auden, are divinities in Brodsky's pantheon.

R. J. Which one of these poets are divinities in your pantheon?

I. B. Among modern poets Tsvetaeva is a wonderful poet, but not a divinity for me. Akhmatova, Pasternak, Blok are. And Auden. It's difficult, I think hopeless, to try to explain why someone likes a poet, and someone else doesn't. Stephen Spender's poetry speaks to me very directly and deeply. So does Yeats. Eliot is a great poet but that is a very different story.

R. J. Are there any English poets that you like?

I. B. I've just told you—there are English poets that I love—but I love Russian poets more, because it's my first language and I think poetry has to be in the language which one spoke as a child. The closest poetry to one is the language which one spoke before the age of ten.

R. J. I was reading a month ago, one of the essays of Czeslaw Milosz on Pasternak. As a matter of fact Milosz considers Pasternak's poetry as an anti–intellectualist poetry. Do you agree with him?

I. B. No, although I know what he means. Pasternak was deeply influenced by the lectures of Hermann Cohen in Marburg. Like Blok, he had read Kant and some of the German metaphysicians and derived something from them. What other modern writer would have mentioned Schelling in a novel as Pasternak mentions him in *Doctor Zhivago*? I think Pasternak understood certain kinds of philosophy very well, and it enters his vision. He was a deeply intelligent, very perceptive man, not at all naive. There are stupid poets who are very gifted, but he was not one.

R. J. Can you give an example of a stupid poet?

I. B.   There is a French poet called Francis Jammes, who I think is a stupid poet. He had a gift for poetry, but intelligent I would not call him. It's rather like what Mazzini once said. Someone said to Mazzini: "What is your opinion of General Garibaldi?" He said: "Have you ever been in a zoological garden?" "Yes." "Have you ever seen a lion?" "Yes." "Would you say that a lion has a very intelligent expression on his face?"

R. J.   Can we go back to Pasternak?

I. B.   I remember I once wrote a short essay on Pasternak which appeared in English in a little collection of pieces edited by an excellent scholar—Victor Erlich, a professor at Yale. He thought it was quite good, although I did not. It was on the dynamism of Pasternak's poetry, where in fact everything is vitalistic, all the metaphors are taken from living beings in nature, nothing is inanimate, everything is filled with force, inanimate objects—tables, chairs, rocks, valleys, colours, shapes, are all seen in an interplay of continuous, vital movement.

R. J.   What made you write that essay?

I. B.   I was commissioned to deliver a lecture in memory of a Slavic scholar. I am like a taxicab—I don't move unless summoned.

R. J.   You told me that you liked Brodsky very much.

I. B.   Very much. He is certainly the greatest Russian poet living now.

R. J.   Well, Brodsky was recently in Paris and he gave a lecture on the essence of poetry. From his point of view, poets can answer questions which scientists and philosophers cannot. Do you agree?

I. B.   Probably. He is usually right.

CHURCHILL, WEIZMANN, NEHRU

R. J.   Now I wish to ask you a few questions about Churchill. Did you ever meet Churchill?

I. B.   Yes I did, after the war. He invited me to lunch. He once made a mistake, when he wanted to invite me during the war in 1944, to talk about America, because I was supposed to be an expert on American political life but instead of me, Irving Berlin, the famous composer, was asked to lunch, and that led to comical misunderstandings— so he thought it was right to invite me after all.

R. J.   And did you meet him again?

I. B.   I met him once or twice at other people's tables but not more than that.

R. J.   You say of Churchill that he had a strong and comprehensive historical imagination?

I. B.   His imagination was a little like that of a schoolboy. For him some nations are historical, others not. Hegel, of course, says that too, but I feel sure that Churchill did not know that. For him Germans are an historical people, so are the French and the Italians and Chinese and Americans perhaps because his mother was an American, so are Jews, but Arabs, Africans, Latin Americans, are not.

R. J.   You say also that Churchill had a romantic vision in foreign affairs.

I. B.   Certainly. By romantic I meant that he had idealized images of countries, of cultures and of what they were and could become and this did not rest on careful empirical observation. The genius of France, the genius of Germany, the genius of England, the genius of Rome, of Greece, of Judaea—idealized patterns of this kind.

R. J.   You also consider Chaim Weizmann a romantic figure.

I. B.   Anybody who could conceive and create a new people out of scattered members of a religious community or race after more than two thousand years must have a romantic imagination. It's certainly a challenge to realism, and yet Weizmann, so far as I know, was deeply realistic. But he understood something very real about the Jews, namely that few human beings in the end want to remain members of a minority in every society. He understood instinctively that people can only develop freely (as Herder thought, of whom Weizmann, so far as I can tell, had never heard) in a country in which they are not perpetually uneasy about what other people think about them, how they look to others, does their behaviour attract unfavourable or perhaps too much attention—are they accepted? Is it all right?

R. J.   As you say, Weizmann was not frightened of the future?

I. B.   No, he and Churchill were both people who were not frightened of the future. They were both strong and confident. They said, "Let the future come, we will do something with it." Never retreat, always *avanti*.

R. J.   You consider both Weizmann and Churchill to have been great men.

I. B.   For me a great man is a man in public life, is one who deliberately causes something important to happen, the probability of which seemed low before he took up the task. A great man is a man who gives history a turn which it could scarcely have taken without him. They give history a twist which nobody would have predicted.

R. J.   Whom do you consider a great man in today's mould?

I. B.   Great men can be very bad men. Stalin in my sense was a great man. He was one of the very worst men who ever lived, but he made of Russia something which would not have happened without him, even if the result was appalling. So were Hitler, Mao, and other monsters. De Gaulle was a great man of a kind. He made a permanent difference to France; but he was a human being unlike the others. Great men leave permanent effects.

R. J.   Do you consider Gandhi and Nehru to have been great men?

I. B.   Yes, I do. I met Nehru. I was in India; I had a friend in the Indian government, who was in Oxford with me, who invited me to deliver a lecture and suddenly Nehru sent for me. We talked together about Russia and England. He talked very well about these subjects. He said that the reason why he had a preference for Russians, although he went to school and university in England and was happy there, and admired the English, was because the English, however public-spirited and benevolent, nevertheless couldn't help patronizing Indians a little. The Russians were crude and barbarous, but they were not superior. That was the difference. Finally, he said that Russians did not make Indians feel beneficiaries. He felt this even about the Japanese. He said, "You can imagine my feelings about the Japanese who were militaristic, imperialistic, Fascists, who did terrible things in the war, and yet when I went to Japan, I felt they were brothers, and I can't feel that about the English."

R. J.   And did you speak of Gandhi with Nehru?

I. B.   No.

R. J.   So you consider Nehru a great man?

I. B.   Yes. Gandhi was an even greater man, because he really created a nation, so did Nehru: Nehru gave to the Indians an image of themselves which I don't think others might have succeeded in doing.

R. J.   In your essay on Weizmann, you claim that he was very much against violence.

I. B.   Very much. He hated it. That's why he was totally against Jewish violence in Palestine.

R. J.   What would have happened if he lived today?

I. B.   Well, if he lived today he would have no power. Even when he became president of Israel, he had no power whatever. He was more or less deprived of influence by his successors.

R. J.   You consider him being against Jewish violence, but in your essay you say that when the Arab–Jewish war broke out his conscience was clear?

I. B.   Absolutely. Because he thought there was no other

way. If you have to defend yourself, if your country is in danger of losing its future—its freedom—you have to defend yourself; then violence is justified. Weizmann was not like Gandhi. He thought the use of force in self-defence was justifiable. He hated terrorism. Weizmann was not a pacifist—he could not have achieved what he did if he had been. But he detested the Jewish violence in Palestine of 1947–8.

R. J.   Do you consider yourself to be a pacifist?

I. B.   No.

GEORGES SOREL, BERNARD LAZARE

R. J.   Do you think violence is inevitable?

I. B.   No. Moreover, I hate it deeply whatever its necessity. Well, I think I told you, ever since I saw a policeman being dragged to his death in the first Russian revolution, I acquired an instinctive dislike of physical violence which has been with me all my life. But still, one has to fight wars. I was not against war against Hitler. The Italians were right to fight the Austrians.

R. J.   Now, the problem of violence brings us to Sorel. What place do you think Sorel acquires as a thinker of violence in the history of ideas?

I. B.   I am not in favour of Sorel's ideas. I am fascinated by him because he is an independent and original figure. That is all; I have no particular sympathy with him.

R. J.   But, why do you consider him as an unclassified thinker?

I. B.   Because he is at the same time on the right- and on the left-wing. He is pro-Lenin and pro-Mussolini. He was for the Church-Militant and against clericalism. He is for and against everything. He was an interesting, mixed-up, gifted man with certain insights and certain absurdities. I am not an admirer, but I am fascinated by him, because he is a remarkable, independent political thinker. That is why I wrote on him. Sorel is a unique figure in the history of French Anarcho-syndicalism. But the man I really admire during that period is Bernard Lazare. You know his history. Lazare was a Jew and an anarchist who wrote the famous book, *The History and the Causes of Anti-Semitism*, an attack on the Jews. The French anti-Semites of the 1880s were delighted by it. At last, they said, there is an honest Jew who sees the defects of the Jews. People like Drumont and Déroulède, and later no doubt Maurras, praised him highly. Lazare (whose real name was Lazare Bernard) was a philosophical anarchist who hated all government. Then came the Dreyfus case. He had nothing in particular to do with it. He didn't know Dreyfus, or his family, but he asked himself why would Dreyfus have engaged in espionage? What motive could he have had? He was rich, conservative, pompous, conventional, ambitious, he wanted to have a successful career in the French army. What could conceivably cause such a man to act disloyally, to give secrets to the German Military Attaché? It was too unlikely, too unintelligible. So Lazare decided that Dreyfus could not have done it, that consequently the only reason for accusing him was that he was a Jew. So Jews were not Frenchmen, after all? Very well he declared, so I am not after all a Frenchman as I had supposed. Some years before he had changed his name from Bernard to Bernard Lazare, evidently because it seemed more Jewish. He proceeded to publish a tremendous letter about Dreyfus attacking the French government and the generals and hoped to be arrested, but he was left alone because the authorities must have realized, I imagine, that they would not gain anything by arresting an eccentric anarchist. He duly became a Zionist, and went to the Second Zionist Congress. Lazare remained an individual figure. After the new French governments of Combes and Waldeck-Rousseau expelled the Roman Catholic teaching Orders to prevent Catholic teaching Lazare wrote passionate articles against them, maintaining that parents and the Roman Church had a right to teach according to their faith; to forbid this was a crime against religious freedom. He died in 1903. I admire him because there is something proudly independent and completely honest about him; he lived a brave and honourable life. I like his courage and his integrity. A very interesting English book on him was written not long ago by an excellent scholar at the University of Bristol—I did not know how admirable he was until I read it.

R. J.   Would you like to write an essay on him?

I. B.   No, because the biography of him by Dr. Nelly Wilson seems to have said all there is to say.

We have talked for a long time—I am sure that you have no further questions to put to me—none at any rate that I could answer.

INDEX OF NAMES

❖

INDEX

INDEX